MW01100521

POSTCARDS
from
IRELAND

POSTCARDS
from
IRELAND

The making of an expat

MICHAEL HARLING

Third Edition
Published 2012, 2020 by Lindenwald Press

© Copyright 2012, 2020 Michael Harling

ISBN-13: 978-1470023676
ISBN-10: 1470023679

Author photograph by Shonagh Buchanan

Lindenwald Press

*Dedicated to the cigar industry
and the Foot and Mouth outbreak of 2001;
without them, none of this would have happened.*

Praise for *Postcards From Ireland*

A laugh-out-loud tale of love, Laundromats, and finding a new life in a very foreign (and wet) land. In "Postcards from Ireland," Michael Harling has once again written a humorous and witty account of how traveling can sometimes lead to unexpected destinations."
**Talli Roland, author of *The Hating Game*
www.talliroland.com**

"Postcards from Ireland" delivers the author's trademark dry humor, but this time with a twist: a charming touch of romance!
**Toni Hargis, author of *Rules Britannia!*
www.expatmum.blogspot.com**

Ireland's charms through the eyes of a baffled American.
**Michelle Gorman, author of *Single in the City*
www.michelegorman.co.uk**

Contents

Foreword

This is a true story. Barring occasional exaggeration for comic effect, all the events described herein happened just the way they are depicted; even the conversations are, for the most part, verbatim. This was happily verified to my satisfaction by the copious journal entries, photos, letters and e-mails relating to the events and the peripheral events leading up to them. These memory-aids were not, however, altogether necessary, as this entire adventure is etched indelibly in my mind.

February 2012

Part I
Searching for
Epiphanies

Heathrow Airport

Ultimately, it was all because of the cigars.

I was several months into an eight-year relationship with a woman I now refer to only as She-Who-Must-Not-Be-Named when I finally took notice of the Tupperware container in the far reaches of the fridge. It had been there since I moved in, so whatever it contained had likely spawned mutant life-forms by now. I pushed aside the plates of leftovers and the untouched bottle of ketchup and took it out. When I opened it, however, instead of seeing things generally confined to Petri dishes, I found half a dozen cigars. The brands were all unfamiliar to me, but I recognized their quality; these were good cigars, not the Dutch Masters or White Owls my father used to smoke.

"I see you've found my cigars," She-Who-Must-Not-Be-Named said, coming up behind me. "I keep them in Tupperware in my fridge so they'll stay fresh; put them back or you'll make them go stale."

I complied, but my curiosity got the better of me and I asked her why she had them; I'd never known her to smoke a cigarette, much less a cigar.

She explained that she and her old college friends used to go camping together once a year in a cabin in the Adirondacks. One of the traditions of that get together was the smoking of cigars around the fireplace in the evening. They hadn't done it in years, but she kept the cigars because she saw no reason to throw them out. So, when we began staying in the cabin in the Adirondacks, we brought the cigars with us and resurrected the tradition.

After that, events escalated at a surreal pace.

We knew a few people at work who were cigar smokers as well, and after a while we began going out in the evenings for occasional "herfs." A herf, we learned, was a cigar term of unknown origin with a versatility that rivaled everyone's favorite four-letter word: to herf was to smoke a cigar, if two or more people met up for the purpose of smoking, trading and talking about cigars, that was a herf. You could herf at a herf, or be herfing on your own, or have a herfable cigar, or…well, I expect you've got the point.

Soon we began tapping into the computer frontier equivalent of Facebook and Twitter: newsgroups. There was a newsgroup for cigar smokers and we became active participants. Soon, our little group began to grow and we started holding weekly herfs at a sympathetic local restaurant where the owner himself was a cigar smoker.

Inexplicably, this same phenomenon was simultaneously taking place in cities and towns all over the country and in other parts of the world. These groups organized themselves into chapters and we established a loose, yearly schedule of herf exchanges, where members of other chapters were invited to the home turf of a local chapter for a weekend of herfing, dining and drinking. These cigar crawls became a matter of pride for each local group as we strove, not to out-do each other (one-upmanship was not part of our cigar creed), but to show our herfing brothers and sisters a good time.

Our chapter name—by a majority vote—became The Herftones, our annual event was ASHCAN (Albany-Saratoga Herf, Crawl and Nosh); soon we became legends in the herfing world, and She-Who-Must-Not-Be-Named became its star.

As you might expect, we considered ourselves cigar aficionados, which meant—in addition to you not wanting to talk to us for very long at a cocktail party—that we were on a constant quest for the world's best cigars. This quest was, and remains, something of a sticking point with the US Government, as the cigars we considered the best originated from a country America was not eager to do business with. But we weren't going to let a little thing like the Trading with the Enemy Act stop us; we were herfers, and not just herfers, we were Herftones, and we would have our cigars.

One of the many ways She-Who-Must-Not-Be-Named overcame this speed bump on the road to herfing nirvana was to cultivate an on-line friendship with a London cigar merchant who was willing to sell and ship cigars to a location that, technically, he shouldn't. Packages from this merchant arrived in thick, padded envelopes purporting to carry travel brochures, which they, in fact, did; the travel brochures contained cigars.

There were other deceptions—some more interesting and inventive—employed by members of the cigar sub-culture which helped retain America's title as the number one importer of cigars from a country that the US, officially, conducts no business with, but they are not relevant to this story:

The cigars from London, when they arrived, were lovingly liberated from the travel brochures; She-Who-

Must-Not-Be-Named got the cigars, I took the travel brochures.

In this way, the petty smuggling of contraband became responsible for me ending up, some years later, in Heathrow airport at 5:30 in the morning on my way to Ireland. The idea of going to Ireland had been evolving for some time and the ads in the brochures about hiking the Irish coast had provided the opportunity for me to turn the notion into reality. Heathrow, however, was my own idea; one of many bad ones, as it turns out.

My itinerary gave me a dozen days in Ireland, including a week of walking with a group from the UK tucked into it. I would have Friday afternoon and Saturday morning to explore on my own before meeting up with the group at Shannon airport, and another three days without adult supervision after we parted ways. My friends kept telling me how brave I was to go off on my own to a foreign country for two weeks, but in retrospect I don't think it was bravery; I was simply too naïve to understand what I was doing.

The first ill-conceived notion I had was that I could pack all the clothing and equipment I would need for the two weeks into a carry-on case and my backpack. This was possible only because I assumed there would be Laundromats in Ireland and that "going for a walk" meant the same thing to me as it did to the tour organizers. To their credit, they tried to warn me. They even sent a questionnaire designed to assess my hiking skills, which I found almost insulting. After all, I hiked the Adirondack trails practically every weekend, conquering peaks such as Hadley, Black, Buck and Cathead. Alright, so most of them were in the low 2,000 foot range but, according to the brochure, the tallest— and only—mountain we were scheduled to climb was Croagh Patrick, and that had an elevation of only 2,500 feet. Compared to the Adirondacks, the gentle hills of Ireland could offer little more than a placid stroll; the planned ascent up Croagh Patrick would be the only activity worthy of my level of hiking proficiency. The rest was going to be easy.

With that thought in mind, I set about preparing for my journey by visiting my favorite Irish pubs, attending an Irish Folk Festival and watching some Irish Dance competitions. I also practiced my own dancing and piping and brushed up on a medley of Irish ballads on my guitar. I even started playing the penny whistle. And just to round it all out, I drank a lot of Guinness.

As an extra measure, I began rehearsing a "Why yes, I *am* a little bit Irish on my mother's side," speech. I wanted it to sound natural, as if I'd been saying it all my life.

Actually, my mother's family came from Germany and my paternal grandfather was born in England, and I didn't think being a Limey Protestant was going to do me much good in a real *Irish* Irish Pub. In the American Irish pubs, I allowed people to believe I was Irish and never told anyone any different. After the clientele put a few pints under their belts and started banging the tables and shouting pro-IRA slogans, things could get fairly nasty at the mere mention of an Englishman. No way was I going to rub elbows with the locals in Cork, Dublin or Kilkenny without some Irish in me, even if I had to make it up.

My packing was undertaken with similar insight and forethought: I stuffed seven pairs of socks, underwear and shirts, along with two pair of jeans, into my newly purchased carry-on bag. I had room left over so I put in a few extra shirts—a mixture of long and short sleeved—and a light jacket. My toiletries, electric razor and plug adapter set all fit neatly into a little travel bag, and I stuffed that in, as well. That was me, done packing.

Fortunately, I had a day or two left to think about it and, on the afternoon before my flight, I decided it might be handy to bring along a second pair of sneakers and a rain jacket. I had to go out and buy the sneakers; the

7

rain jacket—a cheap, bright red plastic affair—I borrowed from a friend. These items, along with a two-week supply of cigars and a notebook, took up more space than I had anticipated, making some last minute rearrangements necessary. In the end, I jettisoned one of the two pair of jeans and all the extra shirts—seven should be plenty.

The next day, toting a bulging carry-on case and a pack stuffed to the breaking point, and armed with a level of confidence that can only be inspired by ignorance, I would be boarding a jet for Heathrow. I could have flown directly to my destination, and, in fact, the travel agent strongly advised that this is what I should do, but I had a plan. I told her I wanted to fly to London, set my foot on British soil, take a few photos of the land of my forefathers and then catch a connection to Shannon. The travel agent looked dubious and told me it would add three hours and two hundred dollars to the trip. I told her it would be worth it and insisted she make the bookings.

My friend Jeanne drove me to the airport so I could avoid the parking fees and not have my car vandalized while I was roaming around the Irish countryside. I hadn't been to Albany Airport in years, and the last time I had flown from there I'd had to walk from the terminal to the plane and climb up a portable stairway. Improvements had been made since then, and now the airport had an actual jetway along with a new name—Albany International—made possible, rumor had it, by the fact that they offered a weekly flight to Montreal.

I went to the check-in desk and was immediately relieved of my carry-on bag. This was a disturbing turn of events. I had, after all, specifically purchased an official airline carry-on bag so I could keep it with me. If I knew anything about international airline travel (and, indeed, I did not; most of my knowledge came from travel-inspired horror stories heard third hand) it was that, once out of your sight, your bags would never be seen again, eventually turning up in Morocco or some similarly exotic location. I didn't tell that to the clerk, but I did explain that my bag met the carry-on standards set by the airline industry—it said so on the tag. She informed me that, because I had over-packed it, it was too big, and she was insisting that I leave it with her and there was no talking her out of it. So, I relinquished my bag, resigned myself to spending my two weeks in Ireland naked, and sulked off to the departure lounge with my backpack. And waited.

The wait gave me time to once again check my camera to ascertain its readiness for the early morning photo shoot. It was an antiquated digital model that could take 45 pictures before the internal pixel reservoir began to overflow, an amount that stunned me when I first got it but which now seemed paltry indeed. Fortunately, a friend had loaned me a memory card that boosted the camera's capacity to an astounding 300 photos. I'd have to limit myself to 21 a day, but I thought I could manage that. To break it in, I took a photo of the departure lounge and another one of the view from the window, where the runways and a bit of the countryside beyond were visible. In about ten hours I would be at Heathrow, looking out at a similar scene; the thought was too amazing to comprehend.

It made me wonder what lay ahead, and if I would really end up getting a tattoo.

The idea that Ireland was going to change me was not a thought I had started out with but rather a notion that had slowly built up over the last few months into a dead certainty which, at this point, I didn't question. Somewhere in Ireland an epiphany lay in wait, one that would solve the riddle of my life. I wasn't sure how this was supposed to happen, maybe the Celtic spirit would call out to me and guide me home, wherever that might be, or the beauty of Ireland would stir my soul into some dramatic realization. Whatever happened, I thought maybe a tattoo would be a fitting way to mark the event.

Something tasteful, and Irish, like a shamrock on my butt.

I didn't tell anyone about this—the epiphany or the tattoo—but its unquestioning reality was reconfirmed as Jeanne dropped me off in front of the terminal. After our cheery goodbyes had been exchanged, she gave me a serious look and said, "This trip is going to change your life." I nodded and said, "I know."

I didn't obsess about the idea—I didn't need to—it would simply happen; of that, I was certain. Besides, they were calling my flight, and obsessing over the flight and the likelihood of making it to Boston pushed all thoughts of epiphanies out of my mind.

The flight to Logan proved uneventful, and there I transferred to the British Airways jet that would carry me across the ocean and I experienced a sudden shift in my perceptions. The plane I was getting on made the ones I had flown across the US in look like toys. It brought to mind a picture in one of my 4th grade school books comparing Columbus' fleet of ships—the Nina, Pinta and Santa Maria—to a modern ocean liner. I had flown in from Albany on the Nina and was about to board The Queen Mary. It was sleek and majestic, glistening under the rays of the setting sun, with engines the size of subway cars and wings large enough to host a southern family reunion on. It was the largest, most awe-inspiring machine I had ever seen; a wonder of engineering that would, I felt certain, drop like a stone from the sky and plummet, in a blazing ball of fire, into the Atlantic Ocean.

Despite the certainty of impending death, I boarded the plane, found my allotted row and sat watching the other passengers stuff suitcases twice the size of my carry-on, along with various bags bulging with airport purchases, into the overhead lockers. I found this terribly unfair; how come they were allowed to bring oversized luggage onto the plane when I was destined to die bagless and without a change of underwear while my

10

suitcase enjoyed a two-week vacation in Morocco? I glared at them all, and consoled myself by imagining them whimpering in terror as the plane plunged toward the gray expanse of the North Atlantic, but then I realized this scenario would have me wetting myself and dying milliseconds after them so, instead, I turned my attention to the wing.

I found the wing fascinating, which was a good thing because I didn't take my eyes off it for the next eight hours. I felt it my duty to be vigilant, in case it decided to do something untoward, like separate from the fuselage or drop an engine. It's not that I felt any obligation toward my baggage-hoarding fellow fliers, I just wanted to be the first to know we were all going to die. So I watched the wing, during a bone-rattling take-off, during the steep ascent, through the cloud layer when the tip was shrouded in mist, into the evening and gathering darkness until just the red navigation light kept me aware of its alarming wobbles and waving, and finally through the rising dawn, as we banked over a snaking river I took to be the Thames and eased onto the runway at Heathrow. Bleary-eyed and glad to be alive, I began to clap; it's what everyone did the last time I had flown and I thought it a marvelous idea. No one joined in this time, however, so I slowly stopped and looked back out the window until it was my turn to leave the plane.

Slowly, excitement began to replace panic. Here I was, in England! The country everyone in my family had talked about going to visit and, except for my uncle's tour of duty during the war, I was the first to actually make it. It was still too dark to get a picture; I would have to take one while I waited for my connecting flight to Shannon. I had over an hour so I wasn't worried, which shows how little I knew about Heathrow and international air travel.

Early as it was, five other jumbo jets landed the same time we did, so getting through customs was like going to a summer sale at Wal-Mart. I squeezed into the back of the crowd and was soon enveloped in bodies as more people joined the crush from behind. We moved forward by inches. I looked at my watch and my itinerary; an hour, I realized, was not going to be enough. Sometime later I was ejected onto the far side of the immigration desks like a pip squeezed out of a lemon. Then I was herded onto a sort of train on wheels, along with a few hundred other travelers, and treated to a ten-minute ride around the airport.

From this low vantage point, the airport looked like a city with really wide streets and big boxy buildings from the Borg school of architecture. I couldn't see beyond the buildings and, even if I did see something worth photographing, we were too jammed in for me to get my camera out. I also didn't have much time: we were soon unceremoniously ejected into another building where we were, apparently, expected to use our own cunning and resources to locate our connecting flights, leaving me just a few minutes to find a window, snap a photo and get to Gate 90 before it closed.

I set off down the corridor at a trot, preparing my camera and searching for a window with an aesthetic vantage point. I was high up now and should be able to see beyond the airport to the outlying countryside. When I found a window, I stopped and readied myself to snap a photo of dawn breaking over England's green fields and spend a moment or two enjoying the view. What I saw, however, was the sun rising over tarmac, towers and taxiing aircraft; Heathrow, I belatedly realized, was big. Very big. The countryside, if there was any, would be miles away. Two hundred dollars and three hours wasted. I took a photo anyway and continued running down the corridor looking for Gate 90.

Inexplicably, I was alone, and the further I ran, the more unsettling this condition became. At length I found someone who worked at the airport, or at least seemed to know their way around, and in desperation, asked for help.

"Gate 90 is that way," the man said, pointing in the direction I had just come from. So I retraced my steps, running just a little faster this time. I arrived out of breath but, thankfully, on time. Even though I was flying a relatively short distance, this was still an international flight, so there was an immigration clerk on hand to wave through all the passengers with EU passports. Then I arrived at the desk, still red-faced and puffing from my sprint down the corridor, and handed her my passport. She studied it a moment, then looked at me.

"What are your plans?"

"My plans?"

"Yes. What are you going to Ireland for?"

In all my preparations, it had never occurred to me that someone might pose that question. "I'm searching for an epiphany," or "I thought I might get a tattoo," were more likely to land me in a secure cell than Shannon airport. At length, I said, "I thought I'd just travel around, you know, see the sights."

The woman looked down, shook her head slightly then gazed back up at me.

"Where are you going to be staying?"

That one also threw me; to tell the truth, I hadn't even thought about it.

"Well, just anywhere, I guess. You do have hotels in Ireland, don't you?"

This time the woman sighed.

"I can't let you in unless you can tell me your plans."

The first tendrils of panic began to seep through my addled brain. I had come this far and now they were threatening to turn me back because…because…I had no idea why, so I asked.

"Why on earth not?"

Another sigh, accompanied by a mixture of puzzlement and pity.

"You might be planning to stay illegally."

I was too shocked to answer. What was she talking about? Illegal aliens lived in America, not Ireland. I stood with my mouth open while behind me people shuffled impatiently and in front of me the plane readied for takeoff. The clerk made one last attempt.

"I'm sorry, but if you don't have any definite plans, I can't let you in." She sounded sorry, but at the same time, she sounded like she meant it. "Don't you have anything?"

I reigned in my confusion and fast-forwarded through the next two weeks.

"Well, for a couple of days I'll be hiking with a group from England."

"Can you prove it?"

I pulled off my pack and began tugging at various zippers.

"I have their brochure, but I don't know if it's in here or my carry-on, and they took my carry-on from me back in Albany, even though it was officially the right size…"

Apparently convinced my ineptitude was not a sham, she stamped my passport and waved me through. I found the plane, and my seat, and stared out the window, amazed at how puzzling the world outside of America was turning out to be. And how small. We were barely airborne when the pilot informed us we could enjoy a view of the coast of Wales if we looked out the window (as opposed to a view of the back of the seat in front of us if we didn't). I looked and, sure enough, there was a coastline. When I had visited Seattle I flew for six hours and landed in the same country, yet we had already left Britain behind and hadn't even attained cruising altitude.

These size differences had contributed to my confusion when I attempted to find the time difference between the west coast of Ireland and Albany, New York. I had searched time zone websites but all I could find was the time in Dublin, which was on the opposite side of the country from Shannon. How many time zones did Ireland stretch across? It took some digging before I uncovered the surprising answer: just one, and it shared it with London. After this discovery, I then spent a half hour checking land masses and was surprised to find that all of Ireland could just about fit into the Adirondack State Park and that England was, give or take a few square miles, the same size as New York State.

I barely had time to marvel over these facts afresh, while wolfing down my second breakfast of the day, before we began our descent. Outside the window, through a gap in the clouds, I saw the famous green and rolling hills of Ireland. Then I began to wonder why everyone kept warning me about the dreadful Irish climate. It looked perfectly inviting from where I was sitting. In fact, the sun had been shining during our entire journey across the country. To my credit, the reason for all the sunshine was beginning to occur to me even as the plane dipped below the cloud cover to land in the gray and drizzling Irish dawn.

Shannon Airport was a cozy little place when compared to Heathrow, much like Albany Airport before the improvements, but with jetways. This, I discovered with some relief, made it difficult for me to get lost. To my further relief, they had my bag, and the crush at customs and immigration was nowhere near as thick or frenetic as the one I had left behind in England.

When I reached the arrivals hall, I exchanged my American greenbacks for Irish punts, or pounds, as they were commonly known. Ireland had signed up for the euro, I was told, but the actual euro currency would not come into effect until January; until then, most prices would be displayed in both euros and pounds and the currency would remain in pounds. I thanked the woman behind the counter for this useless bit of trivia and slipped the wad of unfamiliar bills into my money clip. Then I wandered away to begin my adventure.

Before I could fully comprehend what was happening, I had walked out the front entrance to stand, for the first time, on Irish soil; or, more accurately, on an Irish sidewalk. It was eight o'clock on Friday morning; I had traveled over three thousand miles in thirteen hours. I was, after months of planning, finally in Ireland. And I had no idea what to do next.

Limerick

When I first booked my trip to Ireland, I did so with a solid plan in mind: stay there. It wasn't a very detailed (or particularly rational) plan, but it was a sincere one, born out of desperation and a skewed world view.

I was in year eight of my life sentence with She-Who-Must-Not-Be-Named and would have happily traded places with a Japanese prisoner of war and considered myself to have come away with the better deal. It was a strange situation to be in, because I had no reason to be unhappy; I was living with an intelligent, attractive woman in a tidy suburb with an easy commute to a job I loved. On the surface, those factors should have added up to a high quality of life, but once "The Ketchup Theory of Relationships" is factored in, you will understand how something that looks straight out of *It's a Wonderful Life* (the good parts, where he really does have a wonderful life, not the segments where Clarence is psyching him out) can actually be a thin cover for the "It rubs the lotion on its skin or else it gets the hose" scene from *Silence of the Lambs*.

The Ketchup Theory of Relationships states, quite emphatically, "If your significant other will not allow you to use the brand of ketchup you prefer, then you should leave. Immediately." I know that sounds harsh, but believe me, you will avoid a lot of heartache if you follow that rule. Think about it; you want something, but your significant other is devoted to making sure you don't get it. There is something dark at work in that dynamic, and it manifests itself in the following way:

You're out shopping. It's early in the relationship so shopping is still an exercise in discovery. You get to the ketchup aisle. Your significant other does not even use ketchup. You reach for your brand and pick up a bottle.

Instead of simply allowing you to put it in the cart, a discussion ensues. Perhaps that's not the best brand. Perhaps you should pick a different one, one you don't happen to like but which she insists is superior. This will be a gentle suggestion at first, then made with increasing degrees of vehemence the longer you refuse to comply. Accusations will follow—you aren't doing what she wants because you think she is stupid, or you don't love her, or you're mentally ill. From there—if compliance is not forthcoming—it will escalate to real anger, tears, threats and violence, but you are unlikely to run the full gamut of this argument arc at the supermarket. At some point before the crying starts you will probably just shrug, pick up a bottle of the other brand and put it in your cart. You will think nothing of it, but you have just established the relationship hierarchy, and you are definitely not the one in control.

If this happens, it is best to extract yourself from the relationship as soon as possible.

Moreover, if, after you put your significant other's brand of ketchup in the cart, she removes it and selects an identical bottle off the shelf and puts that one in the cart instead, you should lose her in the produce section, duck into the stock room and escape via the service entrance.

If you don't, you are likely to find yourself, some years later, waking up to the realization that everything in your life—who you see, what you eat, the way you dress, what you read, where you go, what you do and even, to as much an extent as possible, what you think—are all being decided for you.

So when this happened to me, I did the only logical thing I could think of: I plotted to escape by running away to Ireland.

The decision was not immediate; it evolved over time, taking into account my growing love of all things Celtic, my meagerness of job skills and the fact that I can't speak any foreign languages. At the time, the Celtic Tiger was on the prowl and, lacking even anecdotal evidence to back up my conclusion, I assumed it wouldn't be difficult for someone like me—a man with no college credits and a sketchy, self-taught knowledge of computer programming—to get a job over there. I would fly to Ireland and my troubles, even if they weren't over, would at least be three thousand miles away.

I bought a book ("The Idiot's Guide to Moving to Ireland" or something like that), read it during the few private moments I could squeeze from my day and kept it hidden in the secret place where I preserved the last remaining vestiges of who I once was. I don't remember much about the book except that it made moving to another country seem like hard work. It talked about visas and passports and immigration and I stopped reading about two thirds of the way through, not because I was disillusioned with the book or the idea of escaping to Ireland, but rather due to the realization that She-Who-Must-Not-Be-Named would never allow me to travel anywhere on my own.

So the Ireland dream fell to the back of my mind, where it remained until one autumn day when we were at a herf somewhere in New Jersey. The ensuing years had seen She-Who-Must-Not-Be-Named growing steadily chummier with her UK connection, resulting in many late nights in the chat rooms and occasional talk of us taking a European holiday, one that would include, or be limited to, Great Britain. I expect, at that time, her problem was similar to mine: how to get to the other side of the Atlantic without the inconvenience of having your partner in tow. The answer to this came during the cigar party, as she sat chatting amid a cluster of wives and significant others at the far end of the smoke-filled room.

"We've decided the trip to England will be a girls-only trip," she said, turning and calling to me. Seeing as how she considered it a foregone conclusion, discussion was not required, so I merely nodded. Then I said:

"Okay, then I'm going to Ireland."

She couldn't unmask herself in front of her friends, so she nodded in return and my Irish escape route sprang to life.

Naturally, it didn't continue as smoothly as that. After calculations and negotiations, I was just about to book the trip I wanted to go on when she came to me and said, "You don't want to go on that trip. This one is better; I think you should go on this one instead."

Knowing it was pointless to resist, I dropped negotiations for my trip and began researching her idea. After a week or two of e-mails and transatlantic phone calls, I was, once again, ready to book. Then she said, "You can't go on that trip; it's the same week I'm going to England and you have to stay here to watch the dog. You'll have to go on the other one."

So, I booked the trip I had wanted to go on in the first place. And this time, it held, because it was she who had ordered me to book it.

A lot of machinations, negotiations, and money, and all of it unnecessary; by the time the trip rolled around, I was a free man. The end came with a whimper, not with a court order, as I had imagined. Something inside me, some relic of self-esteem must have found purchase in the stony ruins of my spirit and sprouted because one glorious, mid-February morning I opened my eyes and knew—in a way that required no explanation and would suffer no denial, in a way that was physically infused into my make-up, in the way that I knew I was right-handed and had brown (or at least it used to be brown) hair—I was no longer afraid of her.

The strength of knowing meant there was no need for discussion. I said nothing. That Monday I took the afternoon off and rented an apartment. On Tuesday I called in a favor from a friend who owned a pickup truck. On Wednesday She-Who-Must-Not-Be-Named informed me she was going to a cigar crawl in Buffalo for the weekend and I would have to stay home and mind the dog, and it seemed like it was meant to be. On Friday we went to see *Carmen*, performed by a British theater company. The last thing I ever did for her was buy her a small British flag. We got home late. She got up early, packed and I kissed her goodbye. As soon as her car rounded the corner, I called my buddy with the pickup truck.

It wasn't a hard job moving me out. Most of my things were in boxes in the attic, where they had lain dormant for nearly a decade. When we were done, we took a last tour of the rooms to make sure we hadn't missed anything.

"You've lived here for eight years," my friend remarked, "and we just moved all your stuff out but the place doesn't look a bit different."

I looked around and nodded. "That about says it all, doesn't it?"

This is how, eight months later, I arrived in Ireland, not as a fugitive looking for a safe place to hide, but as an adventurer, with my need for liberation behind me and a bold new future ahead. Strangely, standing in front of Shannon Airport holding a bulging backpack and an overstuffed carry-on case, I didn't feel bold, or even liberated; mostly I felt tired and unaccountably confused. It was an airport; there were cars, roads, signs—familiar things you would expect to find in Albany—but they were all so foreign.

I don't recall how long I stood there in the gray morning, or how I eventually came to terms with the unfamiliar road configurations and the backward traffic, but before long I had made my way to a bus stop. This option, and location, must have been pointed out to me by a kindly stranger (or suspicious security guard) because I know for a fact that the idea of taking a bus would never have voluntarily entered my mind. Americans do not ride buses; buses are the province of recently released felons, impoverished students and fringe-dwellers who lack the means, ambition and/or skill-set to own a car. I had, in fact, never willingly stood at a bus stop prior to this, and the mechanisms behind bus routes eluded me. Did I—as I used to do in grade school—simply get on the first bus that came along? How would I know where it was going? What sort of cost was involved? And why do they always post a copy of the periodic table at bus stops?

After a while, it occurred to me that the periodic table was, in fact, a bus schedule and that, to get anywhere, I was expected—without the assistance of an enigma machine—to extract meaning from its unfamiliar and esoteric markings. Then a bus bearing a sign for Limerick pulled up and that struck me as a satisfactory destination—after all, they did come up with those trippy little poems—so I decided to get on.

This wasn't as straightforward as it should have been, seeing as I had a suitcase with me. I wasn't certain if I was allowed to drag it down the aisle to share a seat with me or not and I was contemplating my next move when the driver got off. I assumed he was coming to take my bag and stow it in the cargo hold or tie it to the roof or whatever they did with luggage on buses in Ireland, but instead he rolled a cigarette. I stood on the sidewalk, alternately looking at him, and the bus, and back again until he nodded at me, and the bus and back again. When I didn't move, he mimed opening the cargo compartment on the bus. Surely he didn't expect

22

me to do it. It was his bus, and his job; what if I pinched my finger? What about Occupational Safety? What about lawsuits? He didn't seem concerned, so I opened the hatch and slid my suitcase inside.

A simple thing, and yet strangely liberating. It wasn't until I was seated and rumbling toward the highway that I realized how coddled and cosseted I was in America; every possible threat, every conceivable danger, was covered with foam rubber and hazard warnings. That our headlong rush to achieve 100% safety was in danger of eclipsing our common sense was highlighted by a recent government proposal to erect a 15-foot hurricane fence along the edge of a local overlook so that people stopping to enjoy the view couldn't fall over the cliff. Or see the view. To their credit, this idea was eventually vetoed, but only after a fight. Safety, however, was still their number one concern, and they certainly would never have allowed me to do anything quite so reckless as put my own suitcase on a bus.

The trip to Limerick took about twenty minutes. For much of it, we motored down a road that looked remarkably like an Interstate Highway, flashing past weed-choked verges and roadside trees that resembled scenery I would expect to see while driving in New York, albeit a bit greener. When we hit the outskirts of Limerick, however, I could no longer pretend I was still at home: the streets and sidewalks were impossibly narrow and the houses, squeezed tight together like fat books on a library shelf, sat flush against the pavement, putting pedestrians in ever-present danger of running into a door every time someone checked for the morning paper. And the signs! They were sub-titled in English; the world's primary language given second-billing to a totally unintelligible collection of letters.

Then the bus began making periodic stops to let people off and the primary flaw in my plan became apparent: if you don't know where you are going, how

23

do you know when you have arrived? I had visions of the bus making a complete loop through the city and heading back to the airport with me still on it, so I got off at a likely spot, retrieved my suitcase and watched with a strange sense of abandonment as the bus trundled away, leaving me standing on a street corner in the gray morning rain in a foreign city that appeared to be deserted.

Slinging my pack on my back and dragging my suitcase behind me, I set off in the direction that the bus had gone, making the assumption it was heading for the center of town and that I had gotten off too early. It seemed the wise choice; after a few blocks I began to see people, and a smattering of traffic, though not nearly as much as you would expect to see in downtown Albany at 9 o'clock on a Friday morning. The city also had a strangely squat feel to it; there were no soaring civic office blocks or expansive nineteenth-century edifices sporting gothic spires and frilly facades. Instead, the buildings sat like rows of concrete boxes facing each other across narrow streets, making me feel as if I were trapped in a labyrinth of canyons, like a mouse in a maze.

Eventually, I came to a wider street with a bit more traffic and, as there didn't appear to be anything wider or busier in the vicinity, I assumed I had arrived at downtown Limerick. As if to confirm my assumption, there on the next corner, stood a building advertizing itself as The Royal George Hotel. Jubilant, I headed toward it, only to find my way suddenly blocked by a woman holding a baby.

I had no idea where she had come from; the streets were sparsely populated, there was no one around and yet she had materialized out of nowhere, like a ninja, blocking my way and staring at me with big almond eyes. Her skin was the color of coffee with just a splash of milk and her long black hair was covered by a loose scarf that draped around her shoulders and her peacefully sleeping baby. She was slight and posed no threat, which was a good thing because if it had been her intention to bushwhack me I wouldn't have even had time to scream for help. She held her free hand out to me, then touched her baby and then laid her palm against her cheek, inclining her head as if she were resting. She did this several times and, slowly, I began to understand she was telling me she and her baby had no place to sleep. I must have stood there for over half a minute, mesmerized, watching her, before it occurred to me she wanted money.

By this time, I felt I owed her something for her time, and being giddy with jet-lag and feeling kindly toward the world, I pulled my money clip out of my pocket.

At that time, I had been carrying a money clip for many years, and would continue to do so for several more. It had never attracted undue attention in America and was, in fact, considered somewhat classy, and I never had occasion to regret it. In this situation, however, the disadvantage became apparent the moment my hand—holding a wad of twenty pound notes held neatly together by a gold-plated clip—left my pocket. Her eyes left my face and focused on the money and I realized I was never going to be able to fob her off with a fiver. Still, my mood was not dampened; I was in a position to help and I was glad to do it. I peeled off a twenty and held it out to her.

"Consider this your lucky day," I said. "You caught me in a good mood."

I wasn't sure if she understood me, but she understood the language of money. She took the bill, kissed my hand, bowed, kissed my hand again and then backed away, making various gestures I took to mean "Thank you" as she did. I waited until she was clear of me before continuing on, unmolested, to The George, where I was pleased to find they had rooms available.

The room they gave me began with a "2" so I dragged my luggage up the stairs to the second floor only to find there were no rooms beginning with "2." So I dragged my luggage up to the third floor where, inexplicably, I found my room. With the door shut and locked behind me, whatever reserves I had been calling on to keep myself together suddenly deserted me. I left the suitcase standing where it was, flopped onto the bed fully clothed and fell promptly asleep.

I woke up just after noon, local time, feeling as refreshed as I could expect after going to bed at four o'clock in the morning Eastern Standard Time and getting up at seven. I also felt strangely famished even though I had eaten dinner, breakfast and breakfast on the flights over. I supposed, despite gorging myself on airline food, my body was telling me it was breakfast time, so I proposed to freshen up and go see what downtown Limerick had on offer.

I unpacked, shaved and puzzled over the shower. It was a foreign contraption that needed to be turned on by a pull cord and then adjusted so a trickle of lukewarm water spurted out of the shower head. I had never experienced such an insipid shower; I was used to the kind where the water shot at you like hot needles, scouring the top layer of skin off your body. I did the best I could with it, then considered my clothing options. I had packed enough shirts for a week and was counting on finding a Laundromat after a few days, but I still couldn't afford to waste any.

A quick inspection confirmed the shirt I had worn on the trip over was now out of the "clean" line-up, so I reluctantly pulled on shirt two of seven. After taking care to hide my passport and most of my money (I didn't want to make the mistake of pulling several hundred pounds out of my pocket again) I headed out in search of food, Guinness and Ireland.

It was coming up to one o'clock in the afternoon at this point, and I would have expected the lunch time rush hour to still be alive and well, but the streets were as quiet as downtown Albany after all the State workers have gone home. The only person I encountered was my new best friend with the big brown eyes and the sleeping baby. She ambushed me near the same location where I had seen her the first time, and in the same way; stepping in front of me, making supplicating gestures, pointing to her baby, miming sleep.

This time, I just stared at her in disbelief. Didn't she recognize me? Surely she hadn't encountered any other foreigners gullible enough to fork over twenty pounds that morning, so she must have known she was double-dipping. In Albany, beggars knew enough to only hit you up once. And they were more entertaining about it. One guy used to wander up to unsuspecting people and ask, "Do you have seven cents?" Intrigued, the mark (i.e. me) would automatically put his hand in his pocket, at which point the guy would say, "Or a quarter?" This generally earned an appreciative chuckle and a handful of assorted change. Then the guy would shuffle off and—here is the important bit—try it on someone else. He would never come back to the same person a second time in one day; that would be rude.

But this woman—this pretty and beguiling young woman—did not seem to care. Now, I will be the first to admit I am a sucker for a pretty face, but I was no longer punch-drunk with jet-lag and my sense of propriety overruled (at least on this occasion) my penchant for pretty girls. This woman was not playing by the rules, and I needed to make that clear.

"You already hit me up," I told her. "Don't you remember me?"

In reply, she took my hand and kissed it, and gestured toward her baby. She did, it seemed, remember me, and was now asking if I would fund her child's college tuition.

"No. I've already given you money."

I stepped smartly around her (sometimes you just have to be firm with these people) and hurried on my way, hoping she wasn't going to chase after me. A block or two later, I found a pub.

It had the look of a venerable neighborhood bar with a scarred and age-darkened bar top and a row of wooden stools, each occupied by an old man and each looking as if they had been there since the place opened—in 1847. The atmosphere was smoky, stale and silent. Still, none of the patrons looked hostile, so I went in, grateful for the refuge. I sat myself at the last vacant stool, laid a twenty pound note on the bar and waited for the bartender. I was looking for food, but politeness dictated that I order a drink before ordering food, so I asked for a Guinness.

When the bartender returned with my change I asked if I could place an order and he told me they didn't serve food.

I found this strange. Every bar in New York serves food; it's the law. Apparently I had walked into the only pub in Limerick that didn't serve food. I drank my Guinness in silence, left enough change on the bar for a tip and headed back into the gray and drizzling afternoon.

I turned down a side street, away from the center of town. A few blocks later I found another pub much like the first one, with a dark and smoky interior populated by a bevy of silent, old men. I sat, put another twenty on the bar, ordered a Guinness and asked if I could get some food. They didn't serve food. I drank up, left a tip and repeated the process.

At the fourth pub, a larger one with a more convivial atmosphere, after being told, yet again, that no food was on offer, I asked for a bag of peanuts, lit up a cigar and decided to admit defeat. I really didn't feel like having a drink in every bar in Limerick; I was already woozy from too little food and too much drink and beginning to fear that I might have trouble finding my way back to my hotel. I smoked in silence, wondering what to do next.

"Excuse me, are you a Yank?"

It was the guy two seats away from me, a tall, slim man with dark hair who looked to be in his early thirties. He was nursing a Guinness, one hand wrapped possessively around the glass as it sat on the bar. He had turned to face me and I noted, with some relief, that there was no malice in his look, just simple curiosity.

"Yes, I am," I said.

He took a sip from his glass.

"You're awfully quiet for a Yank."

His name was Joe. He was waiting for his friend, Louise, who was going to meet him after work for a few pints; I gave him the run down on my trip so far, including my visits to the first three pubs and my unsuccessful quest for food. It didn't take long.

"So, just arrived, then? That explains it."

"Explains what?"

He leaned closer.

"Mind if I give you some advice?"

He pointed at the money piled in front of me.

"Take that off the bar. People get their throats slit for less money than that around here."

I hurriedly complied.

"Keep your money in your pocket. When you order a pint, pay for it and put the money back in your pocket. All of it; you don't tip the bartender."

"No tipping?"

"No."

"You're sure?"

"Yes. You don't want to be throwing money around. And if you see any of those Romanian beggars in the street, don't give them anything or you'll never get rid of them."

"Oh. Thanks. I'll remember that."

After the sorely needed lesson in etiquette, we fell into earnest conversation, the kind reserved for drunken encounters such as these: the kind that touches on every subject imaginable, the kind that inspires emotion, makes us sad, mad and glad all at once, the kind of intense discussion that forges friendships, stirs one's soul and, ultimately, means nothing. I recall nothing of what was said, and remember only that we were great friends by the time Louise turned up. She caught up with us without too much difficultly and then the two of us became three, and the conversation continued into the evening.

"I'm in love with him, you know," Louise confided to me at one point. I nodded gravely.

"I thought so," I said, not bothering to add that the way she was leaning up against him with her hand discreetly in his crotch sort of gave it away. Nor did I remind her of the inconvenient fact of Joe's wife. That was beside the point; what mattered was, we were best friends, and as friends do, she was confiding in me. I felt honored; I'd been in Ireland less than twelve hours and I was already one with the locals. To celebrate, I slipped off my bar stool and stumbled my way toward the bathroom, which Joe had told me was called the loo.

Inside, I discovered I was apparently expected to piss up against the wall, because that's what everyone else was doing. A line of men were crowded up along the far side of the small room making like a pack of dogs around a fire hydrant. I shrugged and joined the scrum. A man entered behind me and approached the crowd, jockeying for position.

"Is there room for a little fella in there?"

It was a most convivial piss, and I returned to my convivial companions who, by this time, were being quite convivial with each other. Shortly after, we exchanged heartfelt and enthusiastic farewells and they sent me on my way down the road.

"No, not that way! The Royal George is over there. Top of the road, take the left. You can't miss it."

Once out of sight of my new friends I realized I had never accomplished my primary goal: getting food. Evening had arrived, the sun was sinking low and I was ravenously hungry. I strained to recall what Joe had told me about food, and concluded that it wasn't much. He had told me that pubs did not serve food—something I had, by that time, figured out on my own—but had neglected to tell me how to find any. To be fair, we weren't much concerned about food at the time and my chances of finding any at this point were seriously in doubt. What I needed more than anything was a good long sleep, and I was looking forward to returning to the George to get started on it; supposing, of course, that I was heading in the right direction. I had no reason to believe I was, and the first seeds of doubt were beginning to creep in when I spied a familiar landmark.

She appeared on the sidewalk in front of me, her and her twin sister, holding their hands out to me, touching their babies, resting their heads as if they needed sleep. This time, I was ready for them, I mean, her. I focused my eyes until there was only one of them, then I addressed her:

"Young lady," I said, "this is the third time you have accosted me. I have already given you more money than you deserve, yet you continue to pester me. It's rude, and I am not going to stand for it any longer. Now be on your way."

I still wasn't sure if she understood English or not, but that was surely moot for what came out most probably sounded more like, "shush a fussha waddah, yoush fush gossha puck!"

At any rate, she moved aside, and I somehow navigated two flights of stairs and found the right room. It was only eight in the evening and, for the second time that day I flopped, fully clothed, onto the bed. I was hungry but smiling, reviewing my first, fabulously successful day in Ireland (if success can be measured in pints of Guinness) and looking forward to many more. The room spun one way, the bed the other, and I allowed the vortex to pull me down into sweet, velvet slumber.

Westport

On the 19th of February 2001, I woke up to my first day of liberation from She-Who-Must-Not-Be-Named, and at the same time, three thousand miles away, an abattoir worker in Little Warley, Essex made an unsettling discovery. Several pigs brought in for slaughter from Buckinghamshire and the Isle of Wight appeared to be infected with Aphtae epizooticae, commonly known as Foot and Mouth disease. Over the next 48 hours, more cases were confirmed, and on the 21st of February, the European Union imposed a worldwide ban on exports of British livestock and meat.

In the weeks that followed, while I adjusted to life on the outside and watched spring—both physically and metaphorically—awaken the world with promise, a darkness spread across the United Kingdom. As the disease gripped the countryside, drastic measures were put into action to halt and eradicate it: travel was restricted, virtually crippling the tourist industry, and livestock were culled by the millions. Even one of the pigs that had played Babe in the popular movie of the same name was handed a death sentence (though I understand this was overturned by a judge).

As an American, I was blissfully unaware of this. The only time it entered my consciousness was when the talented young girls from my Irish dance school, who had been planning to go to the world competition in Ireland that spring, were told the event had to be canceled due to the outbreak. I thought, "Oh, what a shame; I hope they qualify next year," and forgot about it. In Britain, however, there was no such luxury. It was on the news every night, tales of distraught farmers, empty resorts and scenes of a countryside that were anything but green and pleasant.

I never saw photos or newsreels of the events as they unfolded, but the footage I watched on retrospective documentaries filled me simultaneously with horror, sadness and disbelief. The livestock were gathered together, slaughtered and huge piles of their carcasses were set alight. Vast swathes of charred, blackened bodies covered the fields, flames danced and oily, acrid smoke rose into the air. It was as I imagined Europe would have looked if Hitler had decided to inflict the final solution on cows, pigs and sheep instead of Jews, gypsies and Poles. Granted, that wouldn't have been quite nearly so horrible, and it would have delayed America's entry in to the war because, quite frankly, we would never have attained the necessary level of national outrage over a bunch of dead cows, not as long as we had our own US Brand Beef grazing on the prairies. And one might suppose that would have been a better strategy for the Third Reich, if it wasn't for the fact that I have already stretched this metaphor too far, so let me close by assuring you that, by the time the Foot and Mouth crisis was over, Britain was pretty much devastated.

The epidemic and its consequences drained $16 billion from the UK economy: it resulted in the slaughter of over ten million sheep, cattle and pigs; it bankrupted farms, decimated the tourism industry, scarred the landscape and left people's livelihoods in ruins. And in the Pound Hill neighborhood of Crawley, in West Sussex, it caused a young woman to adjust her vacation plans because the trip she had arranged to go on in May, to hike the west coast of Ireland, had been cancelled and re-booked for the end of August.

On this morning she was up, earlier than usual for a Saturday, having breakfast and preparing to take the train to Gatwick airport to catch the flight to Shannon. I remained unaware of these happenings, however; I lay on the bed in blissful slumber, ensconced in my ignorance. Then I woke up.

It felt as if someone had poured sand in my mouth, and my head began pounding out a languorous rhythm that made up for its lack of enthusiasm with a grim tenacity. On top of that, I was faint with hunger. The bedside clock said eight in the morning; getting up was the last thing I wanted to do but this was my first full day in Ireland and I didn't want to waste it. Besides, the pain in my head wasn't conducive to sleep so I rolled off the bed and stumbled toward the bathroom, shedding garments along the way. I stood under the trickling shower for ten minutes until I felt as near to human as I knew I was going to get and then went back into the bedroom to retrieve my clothes. It was disquieting to note that I was already on shirt three of seven; I would need to find a Laundromat sooner than I had anticipated, but I couldn't worry about that now. I needed food, and to see as much of Limerick as I could before I had to return to Shannon airport to meet up with the hiking group.

To save time, I packed my suitcase so I would only have to grab it and check out when I returned. Bleary-eyed, tired and so hungry I felt sick, I left my room and went out to discover Limerick.

The weather was still gray and a light rain was falling. The streets, once again, were sparse of people and traffic but, of the few pedestrians around, I recognized one right away. She stepped in front of me, touched her baby, touched my hand and laid the side of her face in her palm as if in sleep. For a person supposedly living on the street, she looked like she'd had a better night than I had.

I held my hands up, palms out, and stepped back.

"No. You are not getting any more money from me. Go away."

I stepped around her and continued down the road, hoping she wasn't following. On a good day, I was sure I could outrun her, but in my present condition, even lumbered with her baby, I wasn't sure I could stay ahead of her very long. After a while, when I didn't feel her hand on my shoulder, I slowed my pace and took stock of the area.

There was a bit of early morning bustle, but as it was the weekend I doubted there would be a lot of people on their way to work and, more importantly, no one stopping to get a bite to eat along the way. None of the buildings looked familiar so I couldn't guess which ones might serve food. I strolled along, gazing into the store windows until I saw some people eating and others lined up at a counter. I went in.

So far, so good, but once I stepped through the door the plan fell apart. There was food here, all right, but how to get it remained a mystery. There was no sign telling me to please wait to be seated, or otherwise indicating what I should do. I tried to watch the others to see how they went about getting served but it was all too baffling and, eventually, I retreated.

My stomach growled in disappointment, but I moved on. A bit further down the road I saw another establishment selling food. I entered, paused, retreated and then repeated this ritual at various eateries as I made my way along the avenue. None of these places looked like restaurants as I knew them; there was nothing familiar to hang on to and no way to decipher the cultural code required to successfully attain food. After the fourth try I gave up and just kept walking, hoping to find a supermarket or even a gas station where I could buy a candy bar and a cup of coffee. Then, just as hope was about to desert me, I saw them in the distance: the Golden Arches.

I made for the familiar landmark and walked through the doors into a little piece of America. Unlike the other places that had baffled me into retreating, this was as friendly and inviting as my own kitchen. It was like a tiny outpost, an embassy and, although I would soon grow to dislike the intrusion of the American culture into the rest of the world, on this morning I might have vaulted the counter and hugged the clerk if I wasn't so tired and ready to pass out from hunger.

I ordered a double-bacon Egg McMuffin with extra hash browns and a large coffee. Then I found a table in the corner where I could savor the meal and spy on the locals. From this vantage point, I could be in St. Louis, Hoboken or any other US city: the décor was classic McCorporate, the staff outfitted with the standard uniform and displaying the requisite amount of lassitude and the clientele were mostly teenagers with slouching posture, poor dress sense and vaguely menacing expressions. Outside it might be the Emerald Isle, but in here, it was red, white and blue.

The intake of grease and salt improved my disposition and the coffee—just as awful in the outlands as it is in America—quelled the pounding in my head to the point where I felt ready to face the remains of the day. Outside, the drizzle had stopped, but the low gray clouds remained. I had no map, no idea where I was, no idea what there was to do in Limerick and no idea what I wanted to do. So I wandered, but always with an eye toward the street where my hotel was; it wouldn't do to become lost in Limerick when I needed to catch the one o'clock bus back to Shannon.

I ambled along narrow lanes paved with cobble stones, where cars were parked bumper to bumper on the sidewalks, I strolled broad avenues that looked remarkably American but with less traffic, and I promenaded the banks along the River Shannon, where the water looked like a stream of sludge and smelled of rotting fish and raw sewage. I decided Limerick—with its stodgy architecture, bland buildings and pervasive, ubiquitous gray—was a dreary place. It lacked the population and endless sprawl to be truly dreadful like an American city, but the dull climate and lackluster cityscape did their best to make up for these shortcomings. Then I found a castle.

I was simply walking down the street and there it was, an authentic castle, taking up valuable city real estate. (In the US, we would have made sure it was in an area large enough to build a theme park around it.) It was the most ancient and magnificent thing I had ever seen. The oldest building ever discovered in Albany was the original fort built by the Dutch when the area was settled in the early 1600s. It was one of the earliest structures build by Europeans in the New World and the fact that it had survived for so long was a miracle. Also miraculous was finding it; a digger accidentally and unexpectedly uncovered a bit of it while excavating an old building site by the edge of the Hudson River. An amazing find, something from which we could learn how the original colonists lived and what life in the 1600s was really like. It caused a three-day delay in the dig, as leaders from our state government came by, had a look and said, "My, how interesting," before building a parking lot on top of it.

It was pleasing to see that Limerick had the foresight to not build a parking lot on the site of their city's oldest structure. Or maybe they simply didn't have that big a need for parking. At any rate, I was glad to have stumbled across it, and even more delighted to discover that, for a reasonable fee, they would allow me to explore it. Without a guide and a safety harness. After I paid my fee, the clerk pointed out that I could choose to view a movie about the history of the castle and, since it was included in the price, I accepted the offer. I was the only one in the small theater and the movie, while mildly informative was a bit, well…I had not yet learned the British term "naff" so I couldn't put a label on the cringing feeling I kept experiencing while wishing the movie would just end and stop embarrassing itself.

Eventually, I made it to the castle proper. The only other castle I had seen was Cinderella's Castle in Disney World, and that one, when examined up close, turned out to be disappointingly small and manufactured from fiberglass. But this castle—St. John's on the Shannon— was immense and constructed from real stones and had real ramparts and walls so thick you could march an army on top of them, which was apparently what they did. I was awestruck at being able to stand in a spot where so much history had taken place. Looking from the wall into the sluggish brown stream below I tried to imagine an assault force docking their longboats in the muck and slogging up the river bank, dodging submerged tires and discarded shopping carts. How, I wondered, if they made it through the sewage and the rotting fish, did they hope to successfully scale these walls?

Not having paid sufficient attention to the film, this was not a question I had much hope of answering, nor did I have the time. I needed to get back to my hotel room, fetch my bags and head for the bus.

I navigated my way through the streets and arrived, miraculously, back at the hotel with ample time to extricate myself from my favorite homeless mother and child act, grab my suitcase and check out. On my morning wander, I had scouted out a bus stop and made a note of how long it would take me to get there. I calculated that I currently had enough time to walk there and catch my bus, but only if I didn't dawdle. So, after leaving the hotel, I crossed the street and took a more roundabout route that was longer but saved time by not requiring a lengthy goodbye scene between me and the homeless waif. I made the bus stop with time to spare, and put my bag in the luggage compartment without being told to.

We rumbled around the city a bit before heading back toward the airport, giving me a chance to see sections I would otherwise not have seen. They were no more inspiring than the parts I had seen but, nonetheless, I was glad for the tour; it wasn't as if I'd be back in Limerick any time soon and, despite the rain and general dreariness, it had been an interesting inaugural adventure.

When I got to Shannon Airport, I made my way to the arrivals lounge, found a seat and waited for an undetermined number of people who I had never met before. This might seem an improbable task, but Shannon Airport was not that crowded and I had the tag identifying me as a member of the group prominently displayed on my luggage. And, as it turned out, I was not the only person inserting a week of hiking into a larger vacation. Not long after I arrived, a soft-spoken and petite couple tentatively approached me to ask if I was with the group. At least that's what I assumed they were asking. The man, wearing rugged clothing and sporting a bushy black mustache, pointed at my suitcase and said something in a French accent, and since he and his wife were trailing suitcases adorned with the identifying tag, I assumed they were asking if I was one of them and not planning to rob me.

They introduced themselves as Jean-Denis and Mireille and I discovered they were, indeed, French but they seemed nice enough despite this shortcoming. We stood together to form a slightly larger collection of people waiting for an undetermined number of strangers and were soon after rewarded with another hit—George and Carol, a couple from Canada, who were also using the hiking trip as a vacation within a vacation.

We were now five, and several things began to occur to me:

1. the group from England, so far, had no English people in it

2. having a structured week had seemed a good idea when I planned the trip, but now it appeared I was destined to spend the better part of my Irish adventure in the company of people who had only one thing in common: none of them were Irish

3. I had not yet met The Single Guy

The letter I had received from the hiking group pointed out that I, being on my own, would be obligated to share accommodation with another guy. Share what remained unclear. I had no objections to occupying the same room as long as the roommate in question wasn't an axe murderer or an Amway salesman. What gave me an uneasy feeling, however, was the idea that—this being a foreign country with equally foreign customs—I might be expected to share a bed with him. Admittedly, evidence that this might be so was based on a partial reading of *Moby Dick*, in which I recalled Ishmael being compelled to share a bed with the savage, Queequeg. That this book was written in 1851 and was about America did nothing to comfort me; on the contrary, the fact that bed-sharing was an old custom in the US made it, in my mind, more likely to have been adopted by the Europeans. And so I was curious about my future roommate, and even more curious about how close we were destined to become.

No additional stragglers augmented the membership of our little band of hikers, and we soon heard the announcement that the flight carrying the remainder of our group had arrived. This was followed by a sudden stampede of passengers as they left the cattle shoot and trampled across the arrivals lounge on their way to the parking lot. I scanned the crowd for signs of our party. They weren't hard to spot; they each had the tell-tale tag fluttering from their suitcases and they all made directly for the Canadian and French couples who had positioned themselves in the middle of the room to act as human magnets. I watched from the sidelines as a couple—the first English couple in our expanding group—joined them. They were followed by a family with a teenage daughter and, after them, came a single guy wearing a puffy purple jacket, sunglasses and a baseball cap pulled low over his forehead. A single woman, older than me but with a thin, athletic build, came next, and close behind her were two older men, one very tall and almost military in his bearing, the other short and wiry. Then the rush of passengers reduced to a trickle and stopped altogether. No one else joined us.

It was me and the young guy, then. It just seemed to me that the two older men should share a room, as they would have more in common, the couples and the family would surely bunk together so the single woman would probably luck out and get a room to herself. That left me and the guy in the baseball cap. I joined the group to take part in the cursory introduction ritual where I learned no one's name but did discover that the guy in the baseball cap was actually a young woman, which caused me to rethink the bedroom line-up.

Still talking and making introductions, we shuffled out to the parking lot and into the waiting minibus, where the couples all sat together and the single people sat by themselves. While the others chatted to one another, I stared out the window, taking in the scenery as we traveled north through County Clare and into Galway on our way to Westport in County Mayo, two and a half hours away.

It had stopped raining for the moment and, on occasion, the sun broke through the clouds, making the green hills sparkle. The landscape was stunning—crisscrossed with stone fences and dotted with sheep and strangely quaint houses—but it all seemed vaguely familiar and I did not feel as if I had yet made a connection with the real Ireland. So far, all I'd done was get drunk and see a castle; the hikes, I hoped, would show me the true heart of Ireland.

After an hour of unendingly fetching scenery, the minibus pulled into a rest area. We were allotted some time to get a snack at the restaurant, which was welcomed news; my Egg McMuffin breakfast was a long time behind me, and dinner was a long way off. However, when I entered the cavernous room I found a confusion of cash registers, random items of food in a scattering of display cases and a swarm of people chatting and clattering and somehow emerging from the fray with fully assembled meals. My group melted into the mêlée and had acquired cups of tea and various snacks while I was still wandering in confusion and becoming mildly panicked at being surrounded by so much food but unable to get any. I could imagine the headlines in the local papers back home: "Clifton Park Resident Starves to Death in Ireland Due to Lack of McDonald Franchises."

Then the young woman in the baseball cap approached and handed me a cafeteria serving tray.

"You'll need one of these," she said. "What is it you're looking for?"

I was starving, but "food" would be too general and anything else too complicated.

"Coffee," I said.

"There's a machine over there. Then you pay the lady at that till over here."

I thanked her and went to the coffee machine. It took a bit of studying but I finally figured out how to make it produce a cup of frothy brown stuff and, satisfied that this was the best I could hope for, went to the appropriate cash register.

As I wandered through the room looking for an empty table, the older guy—the short one—waved me over to where he was sitting with the tall single woman and the woman in the baseball cap. We had already introduced ourselves, but I am terrible at remembering names and I have found it best to admit this up front rather than suffer the embarrassment of having to

43

confess that I don't know who you are even after spending several days in your company.

So they obligingly reintroduced themselves: the older gentleman was Bob, who was twenty years older than me but more fit than I had ever been. He had hiked all over the world and was an exuberant and friendly character. He rapidly became my hero and I didn't think I would mind sharing a room with him, or a bed if it came to that, as long as he kept to his side.

The woman was Judith; lean, with close-cropped hair and a friendly, confident nature. She exuded benign authority and I suspected that, in civilian life, she held a position of some influence, but was the sort of boss you looked up to and admired rather than resented and feared.

Then I turned to the woman in the baseball cap and asked her name.

"That's a nice name," I said, after she told me; then I promptly forgot it. It was something exotic, with a "Shhh" sound in it so, in my mind, I thereafter referred to her as Chiffon and made a mental note to avoid any situation that could expose the fact that I didn't actually know her name.

As for the rest of the group, the tall, older man was Jon, and he was our leader, which perhaps explained his military bearing. Ros and Richard, the only English couple in the group, ran a B&B in Somerset and the family—Margaret, Terry and Lotti—were from Kent, place names that meant as much to me as Clifton Park and Kinderhook, New York meant to them.

We returned to the van and resumed our trip north. And the weather turned gray again.

In the late afternoon we arrived on the outskirts of Westport and an unassuming house where we would be staying for the next three nights, guests of Gerry and Alice O'Neil. The house was large, but still a house. I'd never stayed in a B&B before and I found the accommodation unsettling; it was like staying in someone else's home, which I suppose it is. We hauled our gear out of the minibus and up the O'Neil's driveway where, after sorting out who was staying with whom and where, we moved on to locate our bedrooms. I was, as I supposed, bunking with Bob. Our room was large enough where we wouldn't feel cramped and it featured an attached bathroom and, to my relief, two single beds.

After settling in, we congregated in the living room to review the next day's hike. We were due to climb Croagh Patrick, which was tall enough and close enough that it could be seen from the living room windows when the weather was right. I had to take their word on that because, at the moment, the weather was not right. In fact, it was raining again, and if it didn't stop, we wouldn't be able to do the climb as it would be too dangerous. In that event, a more suitable hike would be substituted.

As you might expect when a group of hikers gather together, talk soon turned to past hikes they had been on and I began to get the first inklings that their version of hiking and mine were somewhat different. I couldn't quite put my finger on it, but they seemed to think a hike involved a lot more preparation, clothing and equipment than I did. I decided not to mention it and, when we were called into the dining room for dinner, talk turned to safer subjects.

After dinner, our hosts mentioned the pub down the road and noted that, as it had stopped raining, we might like to go for a pint. This seemed as fine an idea to me as I am sure it did to our hosts; having more than a dozen houseguests must be off-putting when, after a hard day of looking after them, all you want to do is lounge in front of the TV in your robe and slippers sipping a beer. Half of our party felt as I did and the seven of us ventured into the dark for a walk along the narrow road, relying on Mr. O'Neil's word that, at some undetermined point in the black void that stretched out ahead of us, lay a pub. We walked a distance that, in the

US, would not have been considered without the aid of a motor vehicle, and then walked the same distance again before I saw a glow in the darkness ahead of us that I hoped heralded a pub.

It was called the Sheebeen, a large pub and restaurant with a thatched roof, beamed ceiling and generous seating. I had planned on buying the first round but Chiffon, pressing her advantage of local customs, beat me to it and a pint of Guinness appeared in my hand while I was still trying to figure out how to place an order. We gathered around a large table where I discovered, to my delight, that Terry was a fellow cigar smoker, so I sat with him at the social pariah end of the table where we chatted happily while filling the room with smoke.

He was a builder, from some place in south east England that I had never heard of. Not that it mattered; he'd never heard of Albany, either, and it wasn't like we were going to drop in on each other. He didn't stay long; it had been a tiring day for everyone and he and his wife and daughter left early, taking Bob with them, leaving Chiffon, Judith and myself to have one for the road.

Judith further fed my suspicions that she was in some sort of managerial position by taking charge of the conversation. She was engaging and interested without being pushy and listened without comment as I told her of my adventures so far. Chiffon was quiet and required some drawing out. She was a young woman and a little timid, conservative in dress and wearing no makeup or jewelry save for a silver and turquoise ring on the middle finger of her right hand.

We chatted amiably for another hour, then finished our drinks and set out on the long, dark road home. It had turned into a mild summer evening with no rain or wind, and the scent of the ocean and rotting seaweed was strong. It was a heady, foreign smell that, at last, drove home the feeling I had been waiting for: "Holy shit! I'm in Ireland!"

I went to sleep that night with that thought still swirling through my mind and Bob safely in the other bed.

Croagh Patrick

The storm returned during the night and I woke to the sound of rain lashing against the windows and the sudden realization that I had left all of my toiletries in the George Hotel in Limerick. My toothbrush, toothpaste, electric razor, plug adapters, aspirin, wash bag, comb, nail clippers, dental floss—all of it, left behind. Naturally, I panicked. I did the best I could with improvisation and Bob's kind offer to let me use as much of his stuff that I felt comfortable with (which, let's be honest, was very, very little) and managed to make myself presentable for the time being.

Getting my stuff back became my sole priority, and as I went downstairs to make it the O'Neil's priority, I was no longer worried. It wasn't as if this was the first time I had done this—leaving stuff behind in hotel rooms is sort of a hobby of mine—so I had a plan, the same one that always worked back home: call the hotel and have them send the items to me. We were staying at the B&B for three days; that would surely allow enough time for a package to reach me. I found Gerry and Alice in their kitchen, preparing breakfast for their 14 guests and explained my predicament to them. I wouldn't call their attitude uncaring, but they seemed strangely preoccupied. This puzzled me; up until then it had been my experience that hotel staff couldn't do enough for you but here, the owners of the establishment simply continued to bustle about the kitchen, dodging around me and looking puzzled themselves, as if they couldn't understand why I was telling them about my problem.

When it became obvious I wasn't going to go away and that I expected an immediate resolution to my crisis, Gerry ushered me into the cramped hallway, pointed at a phone and disappeared back into the kitchen. Did they expect me to call the George Hotel? How could I? I had no way of knowing the number. I went back to the kitchen and explained the situation again; maybe they had misunderstood the seriousness. This time there was no hesitation; Gerry—with an apron around his waist, a kitchen towel over his shoulder and a paring knife in his hand—ushered me back into the hall and pointed at a book next to the phone. He was gone before I had a chance to ask what it was.

The book turned out to be a phone directory and, after some guesswork, I managed to come up with the number for a Royal George Hotel in Limerick. So now I had the number, but no clear idea of how to dial it. Was it long distance, would I have to punch in the area code, did I need to reverse the charges? I stared at the phone for a few minutes and, when the phone didn't tell me, I went back to the kitchen. Gerry was chopping vegetables. He didn't turn around when he answered. The tone of his reply struck me as a bit curt, though to give him the benefit of the doubt, he was probably just harried.

Back at the phone I dialed the unfamiliar sequence of numbers and was rewarded with the burring of a telephone instead of a "the number you have dialed is not in service" message. I was not, however, rewarded with someone actually picking the phone up. Granted, it was not yet eight o'clock in the morning, but surely someone would be at the reception desk. I let the phone ring on and, eventually, someone did pick up. I succinctly explained the situation and, because The Royal George was a real hotel instead of a pretend hotel like the O'Neil's, I anticipated a helpful response in return and not a nakedly insincere promise that they would have a look and send on anything they found, which is what I got. I put the phone down and stood in the hallway, baffled, bereft of toiletries and, apparently, destined to remain that way.

By now most of the others were up so I joined them in the sitting room. The story of my predicament had already circulated among them and, while they were at least sympathetic, they were not in a position to be helpful. When Gerry came in to announce breakfast, he told me there was a store in Westport, which was a short walk away, and that they would still be open when we returned from the hike. That had the semblance of a plan and, as I had no other alternative, I decided I could live with it.

Breakfast was a variation of Full Irish, a novel concept to me, but it included things like bacon, eggs and black pudding so I was all for it. It also included things like tomatoes, sautéed mushrooms and, inexplicably, baked beans. Fortunately, each of us was offered a made-to-order breakfast so we could eliminate the bad parts and zero in on the good stuff, which resulted in Gerry and his wife going around the table, laboriously taking individual orders from 14 people and then serving up whatever they felt like.

As we ate, the rain—blown sideways by the gale—pelted at right angles against the windows. I looked outside at the flagpole in the yard, where the pennant snapped as if it were in a wind tunnel. The sky loomed low and gray; the ground was practically covered in water.

"Wow, too bad about the hike," I said. "Looks like we won't be able to go out today."

Everyone stopped eating and looked at me. After a few moments, Jon, the group leader, broke the silence.

"If we waited for good weather," he said, "we'd never go anywhere."

This did little to cheer me, especially as I was on shirt four of seven and only had two pairs of jeans with me, the one I was wearing and the one in my suitcase. I also had doubts that my backpack was waterproof, and it belatedly occurred to me that I had never tested my rain jacket, as if anything would be of help in the storm that was raging outside.

The weather, although it couldn't stop them, was at least a cause for debate. A hike up Croagh Patrick, the local holy mountain, was scheduled for the day, but the climbing trail was not recommended in poor weather so one of the other hikes was to be substituted. Ironically, the weather was so bad that the land the other hikes traversed over, being closer to sea-level, was already underwater, making it necessary for us to revert to Plan A and head for the high ground.

This decision was not arrived at by consensus, but by decree; our hiking group was not a democracy, it was a platoon, headed by Jon, and so we accepted that he knew best and got ready to move out. I kept my disappointment to myself; I had been looking forward to standing on the summit of Croagh Patrick and seeing all of Ireland (well, the North West part of it, anyway) spread out before me. That wasn't about to happen unless a miracle occurred.

After breakfast we retreated to our rooms to prepare and then gathered in the lounge, I in my sneakers, jeans and light jacket while the others donned hooded coats, waterproof hats, heavy boots and long pants with ankle clips. They all stared at me as if I had turned up naked at a dinner party, then we went out to greet the Irish climate.

It was still storming when we piled into the minibus, but by the time we arrived at the base of the mountain it had eased to the point of being just rain. I pulled the red plastic jacket from my backpack, put it on and immediately began sweating. It was, indeed, waterproof but it was also airtight and I felt as if I'd bundled myself up in Saran Wrap, which in a sense I had. I clambered out of the dry van and into the wet day to assemble with the others. They were gathered near the edge of the road junction, next to a sign that pointed the way to three different hiking destinations: Croagh Patrick to the left, and Murrisk Abbey and the National Famine Memorial to the right. The abbey was a half-hour walk away, but the memorial was directly across the road so the group, or perhaps Jon, decided we should go have a look at it.

I knew about the Irish Potato Famine, of course. It was directly responsible for the high proportion of people with Irish last names living in New York City and all up the Hudson Valley, and, therefore, indirectly responsible for me taking the afternoon off work every 17th of March so I could hang out with about 100,000 people of Italian or German or Dutch extraction, to drink green beer and pretend to be Irish. That was about the limit of my knowledge, however, and if I was aware of the suffering that took place in Ireland at the time, I certainly didn't regard it as relevant.

At first glimpse, the monument did not appear to be showing me anything new. It was an impressive bit of sculpting and looked to be a big ship, carrying, I supposed, a load of immigrants to America and a better life. But as I approached, and the occupants of the ship took shape, I realized they were corpses, skeletal remains of starving humans. It was a disturbing revelation, as was the message that, although about a million Irish fetched up on America's shores, an equal number died of starvation, either at home or on the ships carrying them over. In Ireland at the time, people were dying so fast they simply dug big pits to throw the bodies into. Famine pits, they called them; some are marked, others remain unknown. The famine saw Ireland lose a quarter of its population through starvation and immigration and became a turning point in Irish History.

I found this a bit heavy for a rainy Sunday morning. One quarter of the population would mean about 70 million people in the US. What would our country—any country—do if one in four people in the population suddenly disappeared, especially if those left behind were, themselves, at death's door? The whole question seemed too far-fetched to consider, except that it had happened.

We left the monument to the rain and the somber morning and headed back across the street to the trail that led up Croagh Patrick. The rain was still coming down steadily and thick fog was rolling in. My hands and face were freezing but, thanks to my plastic jacket, shirt number four was sticking uncomfortably to my back. I tried to tell myself this is what I had signed up for but failed, mostly because it was not what I had signed up for; I had signed up for sunny skies, green fields, rolling hills and maybe a stroll along the coast, not slogging through rain and fog. What was the point in that? We couldn't see anything? I might as well be on Western Avenue in Albany for all the view I was going to get. And why was everyone so ready to go out in this sort of weather?

As we moved along the level path leading to the mountain's base, I took a closer look at my trail companions. Their waterproof survival gear—from the hats to the boots—was lightweight but looked warm, and the clothing was waterproof without cutting down the flow of air. They also had sticks to help them keep their footing, and the strange, loose pants I had seen some of them put on back at the B&B were waterproof, an item of apparel I had never even heard of before. They were, in short, prepared for this sort of weather and this type of hiking, whereas I was just a typical American in soaking wet clothes and inappropriate footwear wrapped in a bright red piece of plastic.

I recalled the questionnaire I had been sent and the ridiculous questions they had asked and belatedly began to understand what they had been getting at, but there was nothing to be done about that now. I hunched against the wind and rain and marched along with the others. Just as the ground began to rise, at the edge of the path, was a sign warning hikers to stay off the trail on wet or foggy days. No one paid it the slightest attention, so I followed them through the rain and upward into the low clouds.

Because of the bad weather, and due to us being an untested team, we proposed to stick close together on the march to the summit. I thought this was a fine idea, but fifteen minutes later I found myself alone in the fog. There was white to the left, white to the right and white in front and in back of me. Fortunately, I could still see the ground where the trail was clearly visible. I followed it up thinking again about the questionnaire and how I had responded to it.

In my mind hiking, either climbing a mountain or traversing a valley, consisted of a brisk walk over hard-packed earth through benign forests. I'd climbed mountains before, but this one was a different flavor. There was no hard-packed dirt path underfoot leading through a scenic woodland, this was a rocky outcrop, exposed to the elements (and there seemed to be more of them here than I had anticipated) with a slick, stone-strewn trail. I had also never been on a hike where I was supposed to periodically stop and walk in circles around various holy relics. We had been told about this at the start of the hike: for a true pilgrimage to the top of Croagh Patrick, you were supposed to stop at various holy markers situated next to the trail and walk around them seven times. You also might have been required to do this barefoot and backwards while reciting the Apostle's Creed, but I can't be sure; I wasn't paying much attention at the briefing. Nor did I pay any attention to these pilgrimage comfort stops other than use them as evidence of progress as they appeared out of the fog in front of me and slowly dissolved into the mist as they fell behind.

After an hour, the rain let up and I gratefully removed the plastic jacket, giving the stiff wind the opportunity to freeze the sweat on my back, chest and arms and thereby allowing my torso to catch up with the rest of my body. My sneakers were wet through, my toes were numb, my legs cramped with cold. I moved forward again, reflecting that, just four days ago I had been sitting on my balcony, enjoying a cold beer while the thermometer read 104 degrees. I knew I was a long way from home but I was still in the northern hemisphere; surely it was summer here as well.

The further I went, the steeper the trail became and, I had to assume, the higher I was. With only the blank whiteness to go by, I might still be at ground level, walking up an escalator but never gaining any height. A view would have been a good indicator of progress, and a compelling reminder to watch my footing. Slippery trails, tired legs and numb feet are a poor combination and the white bubble I was traveling in impressed upon me that a misstep would see me careening down the mountainside, unseen, in the mist. My absence would likely go unnoticed until they took the next roll call, which could very well be dinnertime. I wondered if the tour company gave demerits to team leaders who returned without the full complement of team members. If so, Jon was taking a hell of a risk.

By now I was moving forward by sheer will power and only because I knew that, if I did stop, I would never be able to move again. My legs no longer felt like part of my body; they seemed to be robotic pistons attached to my torso, stepping, climbing, stepping, climbing, moving me up the nearly vertical rock face, but it had nothing to do with me. Then the trail leveled out and, when it didn't begin to rise again after another twenty or thirty feet, I realized I had arrived. Unhampered by the mountainside, the wind blew freely over the summit, whipping wisps of mist over the barren ground. I sat on a rock near the end of the trail and waited.

I was the first to arrive, or at least I thought so. For all I knew the rest of the group was having a party fifty feet behind me but I'd have no way of knowing. The only certainty was, sooner or later, someone would come up the trail, and then there would be two or three of us lost in the fog, instead of just me.

Fifteen minutes later the feeling had returned to my legs and I had warmed my hands up in my pockets but I was still alone and beginning to wonder if the others—having decided the weather was too bad after all—had turned back without telling me. Eventually, boredom made me brave, or perhaps apathetic, about being lost in the fog, so I took a stroll, being careful to keep the trailhead, if not within sight, at least within the range of my orienteering skills. About thirty yards from where I had been sitting, I found a large white church. It was an impressive size, considering all the materials had to be carried up the trail. The doors were locked but sitting on the lee side cut down considerably on the wind, even if I couldn't get inside.

The rest of the crew began arriving in dribs and drabs, with Chiffon and Bob bringing up the rear. Like me, they discovered there wasn't a lot to do up there, so we huddled against the church wall and ate our sandwiches. Afterward, we set about exploring what we could and found a rectangle of metal tubing surrounding a headstone and a tilting sign proclaiming it to be "St. Patrick's Bed" and not a lot else. Without the satisfaction of completing a pilgrimage or the opportunity to enjoy the view, there was no real reason for being on top of Croagh Patrick.

Chiffon and Judith went to explore the church and, although I had already done that, my social calendar happened to have an opening, so I went with them.

Around the back of the church, next to another locked door, there was a small slot in the concrete wall.

Above it was a sign reading "Offerings." I had traveled three thousand miles, hiked up a rough trail in the wind and rain to see nothing but fog, so I had little reason to feel charitable. Still, I took a pound coin from my pocket, set it on the edge of the hole and let it roll in. As soon as I heard the clunk of the coin hitting the offering box, the sun broke through a gap in the clouds. I scrambled back to a mound on the summit and, as I watched, the mist opened, revealing Ireland's green hills and silver lakes below. It lasted for the briefest of moments and I was the only one to see it.

I guess that's what a pound to St. Patrick gets you; I should have slipped in a fiver.

We left the summit shortly after and, again, were immediately separated by the fog. Going down was easier; I simply had to concentrate on not slipping on the scree. About halfway down, the clouds began to break up and the land below became visible in patches. As the day brightened, I began meeting people on their way up—elderly couples with walking sticks and backpacks, earnest young people who actually did stop and walk around the holy stations seven times and a couple of young girls wearing windbreakers, shorts and sandals and carrying nothing but bottles of water. I felt like a wimp.

I also felt a pain in my left knee. I ignored the first couple of twinges, hoping they were transient and would soon move on, but by the time I reached level ground a lively ache had taken up residence and was already measuring the place for curtains. This was not altogether unexpected—a few times in the past the repetitive jarring of walking downhill had caused one or the other of my knees to get upset—so I had come prepared with anti-inflammatory medication and creams. They were safely stored at the Royal George Hotel in Limerick.

After regrouping again, we walked back to the B&B and I at last found myself ambling through the

Irish countryside. We walked small lanes and farm roads through fields and over gentle hills. The sun was out, the land was shimmering and green and it all felt strangely familiar. Was this my fabricated inner Celt reaching out to Ireland, or the fact that it looked almost exactly like the lanes, farm roads, fields and gentle hills of the Hudson Valley? No wonder so many Irish people had settled in the Catskill area; if you added 87,000 sheep (and the natural by-product of those 87,000 sheep) and threw in a moss-covered stone wall or two, they'd think they were back in Tipperary.

It was early in the afternoon when we made it back to the B&B. We all retired to our rooms to freshen up, at which time I found yet another flaw in my plan. The state of my clothes meant I would have to use shirt five of seven on day four and unveil the second pair of jeans. I decided I'd have to use the good jeans and clean shirt as my non-hiking outfit and keep the now sodden and muddy jeans for hiking. Thankfully, I had thought to bring that second pair of sneakers. The ones I had climbed Croagh Patrick in were soaked through and caked with something I hoped was mud. I cleaned everything as best I could and went down to confirm with Gerry where the nearby store was. He told me to go out the gate, turn right and walk into Westport; it wasn't far and I couldn't miss it.

Right? But that's the way to the Sheebeen Pub, and that's miles. If this store was beyond that, well, certainly someone could drive me, couldn't they?

I said nothing, and set out alone on the quest for toiletries.

It was different during the day. With the shroud of darkness lifted, the mystique disappeared and it turned into a very ordinary road. There wasn't a lot between the B&B and the Sheebeen aside from the curve of the bay. It was long and shallow, half covered in brown seawater and the other half in mud and piles of rotting seaweed. The tide seemed to be ebbing so I expected, when we walked home from the pub in the evening, it would be fully out, which explained the smell.

I walked what surely must have been five miles before I even reached the Sheebeen, then I continued on by, walking at least as long before I saw signs of a town. I went into the first store I found, an Irish equivalent of Rite-Aid, but without as much stuff. My mental shopping list had only a few items on it so I expected to be in and out in no time. Finding a toothbrush and toothpaste wasn't difficult, but when I came to the deodorant aisle, things slowed down considerably. First of all, I couldn't be sure it really was deodorant; none of the packaging looked familiar. I selected a likely brand and hoped for the best. Then I went in search of an electric razor.

I knew I needed an electric razor because I had always had one. It did occur to me, however, that if I did buy one, I wouldn't be able to plug it in back home unless I had some adapters. But I had planned on buying adapters as well because I needed them. I knew I needed them because She-Who-Must-Not-Be-Named told me I needed them, and had bestowed a set on me as a birthday gift, intimating that they were very expensive and precious. Then I stopped and pulled my thoughts out of the grooves that had been worn into my brain over the past eight years and attempted to think for myself. Months of practice had made this exercise easier and, lately, it was seldom necessary, but every now and then I found myself slipping back into one of the ruts.

Buying an electric razor would be stupid, and the adapters were only needed for the razor. And hadn't I seen a rack of them at the airport and been surprised at how cheap they were? I would have congratulated myself for making a rational decision but the entire internal soliloquy turned out to be moot: the store sold neither item. So I picked up a pack of disposable razors and some shaving foam. Then, recalling my previous attempts at shaving with a manual razor, I picked up a styptic pencil on the way to the cashier.

On the return trip, as the Sheebeen came into sight, I realized I was probably thirsty. Besides, all this extra walking certainly wasn't good for my knee; I still didn't have any medication—I had looked for some but couldn't find anything remotely familiar—so a quiet hour spent sitting down with a pint of Guinness would surely be the right thing to do.

The Sheebeen was emptier in the afternoon than it had been the previous evening, but it was still convivial and welcoming and I was glad I had convinced myself to stop. After a pint or two, I returned to the B&B to wait for dinner. Then, after dinner, I—along with most of the group—returned to the pub.

I got the feeling that nearly all of the hikers came out that evening because almost all of them had a grievance to air about the day's hike. Not a big, loud, in-your-face American-type grievance, it was more of a polite, well-mannered British type grievance, but a grievance nonetheless. They all thought climbing Croagh Patrick on such a day was foolhardy and dangerous, especially with an untested group of hikers. This surprised me. Having been willing to go out at all in that weather, I had assumed they were ready for anything, but it appeared even they had their limits.

Like me, they thought it had been a nice adventure that had ended well, but also like me, each of them had found themselves isolated in the fog and mindful of the fact that a false step could easily send them tumbling down the slope. And if no one knew they had fallen, no one would bother sending for help. The couples in the group were able to express this without any loss of self-respect because, really, it was their partner they were worried about. I, on the other hand, having already proven myself a weenie for not wanting to go out at all, had to further discredit myself by admitting that, yeah, it was probably a foolish thing to do; I mean, there was a sign and everything.

No resolution was decided, no motion was made and carried and no vote was taken; we just complained a bit, then half of the group went back to the B&B leaving only Bob, Judith, Chiffon and myself. Just as before, we had a lively chat, and as before, Chiffon tended to sit back and not say much, just like she did at dinner, in the minibus and on the hikes. She was friendly and sociable, simply quiet, so on our walk home, I fell into step next to her in the dark.

"So, you're the quiet one," I said.

And she started to talk. I don't recall what she said, I just loved her voice. The night was quiet and so dark I could barely see her even though she was right next to me, but out of the darkness I heard her voice. It was soft and pleasant, not the harsh, comedy accent of the cockneys, or the unintelligible dialects of the north, but an agreeable accent honed with an edge of authority. She talked of her family, her life, her home in England and very soon we were back at the B&B. This puzzled me; I was certain it had taken me much longer to walk the same route earlier that afternoon.

The Slough of Despond

When I woke the next morning, the sun was shining. I showered, performed an awkward manual shave and then made use of the styptic pencil and half a roll of toilet paper to staunch the flow of blood before putting on shirt six of seven. My knee ached, my first-line sneakers were damp and my hiking jeans were filthy. I hadn't been here a week and already I looked, and felt, as if I'd been sleeping under a bridge.

At breakfast, I heard the good news that there would be no climbing today. It was, Jon told us, a more or less horizontal hike, with just a hill and a few "boggy bits," something I felt I could handle without putting any extra strain on my leg. We were all cheered by the news, as well as the sunshine, but after cramming in to the minibus and setting off to find the trailhead, it started to rain. It managed to not rain hard, or long, but it served the purpose of keeping the ground wet and slippery for when we made it to our destination.

By the time we started the hike, it was—once again—a beautiful day. We walked through a mile or two of what I believed to be the boggy bits—soggy grasslands where the water came up to the tops of my sneakers—and then traversed a forest via a logging road through scenery that looked, smelled and felt exactly like the forests I hiked in the Adirondacks. I began to feel in danger of becoming disillusioned with Ireland; the scenery was stunning but monotonous and I was starting to believe that nothing special was going to happen; this was day five and, so far, the Celtic Spirit had not so much as whispered to me. I had already given up the idea of a tattoo and was thinking that maybe I ought to go with something less dramatic and more easily removable, such as a Claddagh ring, instead. That, of course, assumed something dramatic happened over the next week. If the remaining days were as unremarkable as the previous ones, then it might be best to simply leave Ireland behind when I returned to the States.

After the forest, we came to a blacktopped path and the whole group sat down on its sun-warmed surface. Some took advantage of the sunshine, and the only dry land we had seen so far, to remove their sodden shoes and socks while the rest of us simply enjoyed being temporarily out of the damp. I was marveling at what good condition the pathway was in when I saw a car approaching and realized it was not a hiking trail at all but an actual two-lane road. Our short respite came to an abrupt end and, once everyone had put their socks and boots back on, the hike resumed.

We stayed on the road for some way, following it as it wound around the mountain where it overlooked the most fetching green valley I had ever seen. I stopped and leaned against the mossy stone wall at the edge of the road, looking at the splendid scenery laid out below in the sparkling sunshine. This was Ireland, lush and lovely, and there was no mistaking it for anything else. The sight refreshed me, and reawakened my sense of destiny; but I still wasn't going to get a tattoo.

The weather remained agreeable for the remainder of the day, at least for the most part. I was coming to understand that good weather in Ireland was a relative, and fleeting, concept, but at least it was something I could point to that was vastly different from back home.

For the moment, however, it was sunny and warm and our group marched happily along the narrow road until we came to the base of the valley.

"The path leaves the road here," Jon said, consulting his map. "We cross a stream and then climb over the hill and hike along the edge of Lough Lugacolliwee."

This sounded fine on the surface, except for the name of the lake which I could not even begin to pronounce, but the "cross a stream" comment seemed a bit too glib for me. Even though the stream was far away, across a field and hidden in a gully that ran down the side of the slope, I had visions of a rain-swollen torrent crashing over rocks, lying in wait for a hiker foolish enough to think they could easily ford it. Apparently, a few of the others shared this vision, as well; they pointed to where the road dipped into the valley and a stone bridge spanned the rushing water.

"Couldn't we cross using that bridge and then cut across up the hill?"

I don't know who asked that, but I could have kissed them.

"That's not where the trail goes," Jon said. "I like to stick to the trail."

None of us were as concerned about the proposed unauthorized detour as Jon was, but he remained reluctant to change his mind.

"Is there a safe crossing point?" someone asked. "What have you done in the past?"

"Oh, I've never been here before," Jon said. "I like to explore new areas whenever I take a group out."

That was when it became clear we were following a madman into the unknown, a man who had no idea of the capabilities of his squad, who preferred to lead us into danger rather than take a safe route because "that's what the book says." In America, he'd have had a mutiny on his hands, but our group—being mostly

British—simply shrugged and followed our commander into the valley of death, straight toward the enemy lines.

When we reached the stream, which was, as I had imagined, a roiling, raging swirl of white water and spray, we split into smaller groups and spread out along the bank, each looking for a different crossing point. I suppose the theory was that this would increase the chances of at least some of us making it over and allow the survivors to alert the appropriate authorities, assemble a search party and attempt to locate the bodies of our fallen comrades before they were washed out to sea.

I fell in with Margaret, Terry and their daughter, Lottie. We managed a precarious crossing using their walking sticks to pull each other from rock to rock and, ultimately, to the opposite side. It was a tricky maneuver, requiring steady nerves and good balance to keep from slipping in and being carried away by the current.

Eventually, we gathered at the edge of the wood, a safe distance from the rushing water, took a head count and discovered, incredibly, that we had all made it. Relieved that we didn't need to mount a rescue operation, we pressed on. Then it began to rain.

It didn't rain hard, but it rained steadily, forcing me to don my plastic jacket. During one of the other rain bouts, I had discovered that my pack was not waterproof so I had to wear the jacket over my pack in order to keep my supplies dry. I immediately began to overheat and eventually just wore the jacket unzipped because the rain wasn't soaking me any worse than my own sweat was.

Just before noon we began climbing the hill. As I had hoped, it wasn't as steep or treacherous as Croagh Patrick, but the ground was uneven and rutted, making my leg twist and my knee complain with every step. And so we walked. And walked. And walked. It hadn't seemed a large hill when we started up it, but the top continued to elude us and, when we stopped for lunch, we found we were barely a third of the way up.

The rain began to let up after lunch and we continued toward the top. It was slow going; even after the sun came out the ground remained sodden, slippery and treacherous. There was, I began to suspect, no dry land in Ireland. Even the inviting meadows I had seen had turned out to be no more than soggy morasses of weeds and muck—the Irish equivalent of quicksand or the La Brea Tar Pit, perhaps—with benign surfaces camouflaging their dangerous underbellies. Also, up until then, I had always associated high ground with dry ground, but here we were, halfway up a very large hill, and the ground was still squishing underfoot and running with rivulets of brown water.

At length, we attained the summit and were rewarded with a most striking view. I snapped another of my daily allotted photos and spent some time being awed by the panorama stretching out before me. It was fetchingly rumpled and dappled with cloud shadows. The brownish green of the nearby hills undulated into the distance, merging with the blue of the faraway mountains. Below us, nestled in a wide basin surrounded by smaller hills, the silvery surface of Lough Lugacolliwee ruffled in the breeze. I was pleased to see this; all the brooks and streams we had thus far encountered hiking—and they had been numerous—were all, thanks to the peat and tons of sheep dung on the ground, the color of extremely potent tea, making me wonder if there was any clean water anywhere in Ireland. Even the River Shannon was little more than a trough of brown sludge with a horrific stench, and the ocean along the road to the Sheebeen, where it ebbed and flowed across the tidal flats, was likewise brown, murky and odiferous. Given this, the sight of a clear, sparkling lake was welcome, indeed.

What was not welcome was the sight of what lay beyond. The countryside rolled on and on, with a remarkable lack of houses, roads or any sort of amenities. And just beyond the far end of the lake, an ominous brown stain stretched over the only flat land I could see, spreading like a muddy boot print over the otherwise inviting landscape. This, they told me, was the boggy bit. Not at all encouraged by the news, I started down the other side of the hill.

The descent was quicker, but trickier, than the ascent. Steep and slick, it seemed designed to trip you up and as we marched further into the valley, people slid, people fell, and people—one by one—joined what we began to refer to as The Wet Bum Club. I had to pick my way carefully through the terrain, and this caused my knee to complain bitterly. Chiffon offered what help she could in the form of an ACE bandage and some chewable ibuprofen, but it did little good. Still, I managed to reach the base of the hill and the shores of Lough Lugacolliwee, which I referred to as Lake Louie, because I could pronounce that, without having joined The Wet Bum Club.

We hiked the rim of the lake on flat land that made the going easier, then came to the Boggy Bit. Until then, I had no idea what a bog was. I had thought the swampy grassland we had slogged through earlier was a bog, or perhaps a bog was that muddy patch of ground we had crossed a while back. No such luck; what Jon had been talking about, and what lay before us, was a real, authentic bog—a vast expanse of brown, spongy peat that seemed to stretch on for miles. We regarded it with a collective groan and ploughed ahead.

It was firmer than it appeared—which was fortunate or we all would have disappeared into the mire—but that didn't change the fact that it felt like we were walking on a sopping, brown sponge. The only way across was to put on foot ahead of the other. And this I kept doing.

Eventually, due to my knee, I fell to the rear of the group with the rest of the walking wounded. We moved forward in silence, one step at a time, with no energy wasted on conversation. All we had to offer to keep each other's spirit up was our proximity, as we watched the distance between us and the lead group grow longer and longer. After what seemed an eternity we emerged, only to find even more wet and treacherous grasslands. Crossing this expanse was similar to a military expedition into enemy territory, where the point man would warn of danger ahead by stumbling into an ambush or stepping on a land mine. In similar fashion, we walked in single file, keeping an eye on the point man. At regular intervals, the point man (or woman) would disappear from view, and we would hear the cry, "Hole!" or "Slippery bit!" The point man would then join The Wet Bum Club and the rest of us would avoid the hazard.

In this way we traversed the field. Near the far end, tantalizingly close to the road out, we came up against what can only be described as a small pond with grass growing in it. There was nothing to be done but slog through it. This turned out to be a good thing, however, as our feet couldn't really get any wetter at that point and it served to clean off our shoes and boots.

From there we had a few fences to clamber over and then we found ourselves on a broad path that led to a narrow road. Our journey was supposed to take us another mile or three along that road but our driver did us a kindness and drove in to pick us up. We were an hour behind schedule, so it was to his advantage as well. Despite this not being the official end of the hike, we were all—even Jon—glad to get in the van.

Back at the B&B I took a shower and changed into my last clean shirt. Bob gave me some of his pain medication and Judith loaned me a tube of anti-inflammatory cream which did little to help.

At dinner, discussion centered on the hike and the next day's offering, which was a thirteen and a half mile trek. Most people were still marveling, but not in an admiring way, that I was hiking in sneakers, which they referred to as trainers. I suspect they thought it served me right to have developed a sore knee; the idea of going hiking in such a woefully unprepared condition was inconceivable to them, just as taking it so seriously was inconceivable to me. I was certainly a poor influence on the group; during the meal, instead of joining the discussion, I encouraged Lottie and Chiffon to see which of us could curl our tongues, cross our eyes and flip their eyelids inside out. To his credit, Jon never said, "If you kids can't behave you can leave the table," but I suspect he wanted to.

After dinner, most of the group went in to Westport while Judith, Chiffon and I returned to the Sheebeen. We had definitely formed our own little cadre and I was glad for this. They were easy company, interesting to talk to and I felt comfortable with them even though they were women. During those tumultuous days with She-Who-Must-Not-Be-Named, I came to the conclusion that I was not cut out for long term relationships and had told my friends, "If I ever get out of this alive I am going to hire a guy to follow me around and kick me in the ass any time I look twice at a woman." In the months since I had escaped, that had worked very well for me. I had women acquaintances, but I was careful to keep any cross-gender relationships squarely in the "friends" arena. With Judith and Chiffon, I didn't need to be so guarded, as the chances for emotional attachment were non-existent, and this made being in their company a lot more relaxing.

On this evening, after discussing at length how miserable the hikes had been, I told them that, because my leg was aching so badly, I was thinking of giving the next day's march a miss. I thought taking it easy for a day would set everything right and allow me to enjoy the rest of the hikes. They agreed that would probably be a good idea, though I expect they were thinking that some appropriate hiking gear would better allow me to enjoy the rest of the hikes.

As we walked back to the B&B that evening, however, it wasn't my knee or the upcoming hikes I was worried about; I was more concerned about what I was going to wear the next day.

The Wimpy American

On the sixth day of my vacation I was officially out of shirts. Truth be told, I'd been out of pants since the second day; rotating my two pairs of jeans—one for hiking and one for socializing—worked fine for a day or two, but now even my good pair were showing the strain. At least I still had clean socks and underwear, but I was going through socks faster than I had planned and my supply of underwear—even if I continued to avoid taking up membership in The Wet Bum Club—could only hold out until Friday.

These were the thoughts that occupied me as I stared at my face in the bathroom mirror, dabbing at the numerous cuts with my styptic pencil. With my clothing options limited, I couldn't afford to bleed on anything. Satisfied that my face had stopped leaking, I selected my cleanest dirty shirt and hobbled downstairs for breakfast. My fashion forecast was looking as bleak as the weather, but at least I had a plan.

Breakfast, despite the rain rattling against the windows like machine gun fire, was fairly upbeat, but this had more to do with the service than the prospect of walking into the gale. As she did every morning, Mrs. O'Neil greeted us all and took 14 individual orders. She then went into the kitchen and emerged sometime later with whatever she happened to cook up that morning. This daily ritual was the cause of much mirth, and with the dreary weather, we took our mirth where we could find it. The mood remained light until I told Jon I wasn't going on the hike.

I was glad I had thought to mention this at the pub the previous night; it kept me from looking as if I had wimped out due to the weather, and it encouraged Judith and Chiffon to speak up in favor of my idea and my reasoning. With their support, Jon accepted my decision. He had no choice; it was either leave me behind or force me on the march with a gun to my back, something I suspect he would secretly have enjoyed.

With the issue settled and breakfast over, I bid the group goodbye and good luck, thanked Judith and Chiffon (whose name, I was beginning to suspect, was not Chiffon) and retired to my room to plan out my day. I had two goals in mind; find a Laundromat and take a side trip to Ballina. This side trip was inspired by my growing realization that Ireland was a relatively small place and that a guy I used to know from a local band called Donnybrook Fair had moved to Ireland and was running a pub there. I gave that adventure a 50-50 chance of success as it required renting a car, finding Ballina and locating the correct pub. The Laundromat, in my mind, was a sure bet; Westport was a large town so there would surely be someplace to do laundry.

I watched the minibus take the group into the storm for their appointed hike, mentally high-fiving myself for finding a way of avoiding it. What good would hiking in that weather do? It was bad enough I had to go into town, and I certainly wasn't going to walk. I used the B&B phone to call a cab and half an hour later I was in the center of Westport, wandering the windblown streets looking for a place to rent a car. To my surprise, I actually found one, but the man behind the counter said they were fresh out of cars. I didn't press the issue, or ask if there was another place I could try; the idea of driving around the countryside, with the wind blowing and the rain hammering, looking for a town where a guy

I used to know might or might not live suddenly seemed not such a good idea after all.

Unfortunately, walking around town looking for a Laundromat wasn't a much better idea. There were none to be had and, after half an hour of fruitless searching I ducked into a shop to buy an umbrella so I could at least remain semi-dry while completing my fool's errands. I found a good-sized, sturdy, black model that turned into an inverted cone the moment I stepped onto the sidewalk. After man-handling the mangled umbrella into a trash can, I wandered around for a bit more, enjoying the relative solitude of the streets. When I decided I couldn't get any wetter, I went into what looked to be a department store where I purchased some pain medication and my own ACE bandage so I could give Chiffon back the one I was currently wearing.

At some point during the previous evening, I had heard someone call Chiffon by name, and it sounded more like Cha vawn', which, I understand, is spelled Siobhán. No matter; I didn't need to write it down anywhere and I wasn't confident enough to say it out loud, to her or anyone else in the group. With my knack for getting names mixed up, her actual name was probably Gertrude, but I filed Siobhán away, just in case.

Having purchased something useful, I got into the mood, and wove my way into and out of additional shops to pick up a few mementoes and gifts for my three boys. I was going to get them each a shirt with something silly on it, but I figured that they—being semi-adults—were probably tired of my sense of humor, so I bought three quality golf shirts each bearing a tasteful Guinness logo. With my shopping craving satisfied, I found a restaurant and had a solitary lunch of Irish stew.

Then a strange thing happened; the sun came out.

I hadn't realized how long it had been since I had experienced really nice weather, but emerging from the darkened restaurant to the blinding light of the outdoors was as shocking as it was welcomed. I wandered the town anew, looking at it in the sunshine and deciding I liked it a lot better that way. So did everyone else. With the agreeable weather came hordes of people who must have been hiding in cellars and attics until then because there were literally more of them than could comfortably fit in the town.

It wasn't long before I found myself being squeezed off the sidewalks and having problems crossing roads because of the sudden influx of cars. And the languages; all around me I heard the babble of voices but not one of them was speaking English. I heard German, Spanish and some sort of oriental dialect but nothing I could comprehend. Being surrounded by people I couldn't understand so far from home made me suddenly lonely and, ironically, I began to wish the storms would return so all these people would go back to where they had been hiding and allow me to enjoy the serenity of the streets again.

Eventually, tired of being jostled, I called a taxi to take me, and my purchases, back to the B&B. I knew where the B&B was, and even the name of the road, but that didn't seem to satisfy the man on the other end of the phone.

"Where is it you're wanting to go, then?" he kept asking, and I would explain the approximate location. Then, finally, he said, "Oh, you're talking about Gerry O'Neil's place. I'll be right by to pick you up."

And he was. And I didn't need to give him directions because he appeared to know Gerry, and seemingly everyone else in County Mayo, by name. This was apparently how he—and, for all I knew, the entire population of Ireland—got around, not with a map, but by knowing where everyone lived.

I had him wait while I stashed the booty in my room and told the O'Neils that, as I had not found a Laundromat, I would not be making any more trips back to their house, leaving them free to tidy up, prepare for dinner, have animal sex on the dining room table, or whatever it is they do when their house is not full of guests. It did seem a bit strange that they didn't offer to help me out with my laundry woes. Even if they weren't going to offer to do a load for me (which, in America, I would simply expect and offer to pay for) they could at least point me in the direction of the nearest laundry facility. But they simply listened, silently and without sympathy and, more to the point, with no offer of help. Perhaps they were secretly enjoying my plight, and viewed it as payback for making such a nuisance of myself over my lost toiletries that first morning. That, at least, was an attitude I could understand.

Back in the cab, I told the driver to take me to the Sheebeen pub. Fortunately, he didn't ask me who owned it, he just drove me the short way down the road and dropped me in the parking lot without so much as a quip about lazy Americans who can't be bothered to walk. For this, I gave him a generous tip.

By now I was becoming comfortable with the Sheebeen. I knew the bartender by sight, if not by name, and he knew my drink was Guinness. I sought out my favorite booth and sat in solitude to soak up the atmosphere. The cavernous room, even with the sun shining through the windows, remained dim, the light muted by the rough-hewn beams and weathered wood. Being early in the day, it was quiet, almost empty, the perfect place for a thoughtful cigar and refreshing pint.

I was fortunate to have this opportunity, because this was to be our last night at the B&B. After the next day's hike, we would be taken to another hotel—the Connemara Gateway in County Galway—which the people in the group had described as "posh," meaning, they explained, that it was very nice. This was not unwelcome news to me—the fact that we were moving on, that is, not the condition of our next hotel—for I had had enough of Westport. In truth, I felt I had had enough of Ireland; after a day of travel and five full days "in country" all I had managed to do was run out of clean clothes. There was no magic here, nothing that was going to change my life and I wasn't going to discover the spirit of Ireland; I'd be lucky enough to find a laundry. Perhaps my disappointment stemmed from expecting too much, but so far it felt like traveling in America, only with funny accents and monopoly money. If I were going home the next day instead of to the posh hotel, I would not have felt cheated.

What I had mostly seen in Ireland, so far, was people from other countries. I spent the day hiking with Brits, Canadians and a French couple, and had seen all manner of nationalities in Westport, but so far had engaged in no meaningful interaction with real Irish people. Joe and Louise almost fit the bill, but "meaningful interaction" in my book meant sober, or at least something you could remember. The O'Neils didn't count either, as they didn't interact much. I had never stayed in a B&B before and I was looking forward to never staying in one again. Overall, it had the same flavor as a trip to a distant relative's house, or sleeping over with the friend of a friend—awkward, inconvenient and slightly embarrassing.

I stayed for another pint and cigar, making them stretch out as long as I could; I didn't want to return to the B&B before the group but I also didn't want to show up three sheets to the wind. When I felt it was safe to impose myself on the O'Neils I walked back, noting that my knee, although better, was still whining like a spoiled child over the inconvenience of motion. I ignored it; it was just being a slacker.

The group, I was pleased to note, had already returned and was in the collective process of cleaning themselves up for dinner. I sat alone in the living room and waited.   One by one they made their way downstairs, looking none the worse for having spent the morning out in the storm.   When Siobhán came down, I asked how the hike was. "Bracing," she said. I liked that; it sounded very English.

I had to admit the group was holding up very well. They continued to be cheerful in the face of adversity and, despite our secret bitch-sessions, no petty squabbles had arisen so far, though for seven days, I expect most anyone can force themselves to get along.   Jon, admittedly, was something of a martinet, but if there was a weak link, it was me.

At dinner the talk was, as usual, of the next day's hike and, as usual, there were the predictions that, if the weather didn't improve, it would have to be changed. By now I was coming to understand that Jon was as likely to alter The Plan as I was to suddenly conjure up weather-appropriate clothing; we would go on the planned hike come hell or high water, and—in my sopping sneakers and muddy jeans—I was certain to run into one or the other.

After dinner the group dispersed again, some to the Sheebeen, others into Westport to explore the town, and the cadre of singletons—Judith, Siobhán, Bob and myself—went to see a play. It was called *Thy Will Be Done* and was put on in the town hall by a local company, meaning the audience and the actors were all Irish.   The play was forgettable—as evidenced by the fact that I had no idea what it was about, other than there seemed to be a lot of flying back and forth to America and I thought that would be a tad expensive—and the acting was merely passable, but the thrill of doing something normal, along with an auditorium full of other normal people, made me feel a little closer to this elusive country.   By the end of the play, I felt more kindly, and hopeful, about Ireland than during the afternoon.   Then, afterwards we went for a drink, and that made me feel even more kindly.

The weather was still agreeable so we chose Horan's Pub, which had a courtyard where we could sit outside and enjoy the twilight. It was a grand evening in late summer, I was at a pub, with people who, if they weren't friends, were at least nice company, and I was drinking a Guinness; an Irish Guinness, at that. I had not yet arrived (I was with English people, after all) but I was getting closer and I allowed the feeling of comfortable companionship to wash over me. Siobhán remained quiet while Bob, ever effervescent, and Judith did most of the talking. Judith, who seemed strangely knowledgeable about local history, told us that the pub we were at was owned by Matt Malloy, one of the Chieftains. Having explored Westport earlier in the day, I suggested that Matt Malloy's pub might actually be the pub called Matt Malloy's Pub on the next street.

But being Ireland, we couldn't really be sure.

The Death March

A s I shaved the next morning, it looked as if the fine weather was holding out. I wished I could say as much for my face; the few days of scraping a razor over it had left my cheeks sore, puffy and accruing an impressive collection of tiny scabs. It would be nice to give shaving a miss for a day or so, but Jon didn't strike me as the sort of commander who tolerated untidiness among his troops. Besides, I didn't want Siobhán and the others thinking I was slovenly as well as inept at packing. I was a little concerned about that last item. I was totally out of shirts, my jeans were holding up heroically but they were in definite need of a washing machine and, after putting on my underwear, I was dismayed to see I had only two pair left. We would be leaving the B&B today and staying the night in a hotel; I could only hope they had a laundry.

That, however, would not help me now. I had already worn my cleanest dirty shirt, and number two was not going to cut it. I dropped the bulging wash-bag in my suitcase and eyed the bag containing my purchases from the day before. Maybe I could buy the boys something else later on, I thought, taking out one of the shirts. My children were, at that time, all hovering around the big two-oh—a set of twins and another one that hurried along after—and were all, fortuitously enough, my size. I took the shirt out of its package and put it on, thinking it was also fortunate I had decided against a joke gift: I didn't fancy hiking the hills of Galway wearing "Kiss me, I'm Irish" or "Erin go BRA-less" plastered across my chest.

The talk at breakfast was, of course, about changing the hike. The weather was agreeable enough at the moment, but that was expected to change—no surprise there—and even if it didn't, the water level would surely be above average over the next week or so. In the end, Jon decided to stick to The Plan; we would march the prescribed route, enemy guns be damned. We all went back to our rooms to pack, write our final letters home, contemplate life and whatever else you do on the eve of a big battle.

The day of rest had done my knee a big favor, but it was still nowhere near back to normal. I took some pain killers, rubbed the anti-inflammatory cream on it, wrapped it in the ACE bandage and hoped for the best. The bundle of dirty laundry nearly took up the entire suitcase, leaving barely enough room for my clean sneakers and no room at all for my purchases. I stuffed my plastic rain jacket into my pack along with my other hiking essentials, laid the bag of souvenirs on top of the suitcase and hoped everything would still be in it when it got to wherever it was going.

There were hugs and handshakes as we piled into the van and drove away from the B&B for the final time. I for one was looking forward to staying in a proper hotel. So was Judith, apparently; she had booked herself a single room at the Connemara Gateway, just in case, I supposed, that her roommate turned out to be an insufferable jerk or a lesbian or something. Siobhán didn't seem to be a lesbian, and she certainly was not an insufferable jerk—in fact, she and Judith were getting on very well—but Judith figured she'd take the room anyway, just to give them a chance to get away from each other. I had to admire her proactive nature; I had been worried about the sleeping arrangements but hadn't had the foresight to do anything about it. On the other hand, if Bob had been amorously inclined toward me, having a spare room at this juncture wouldn't do much good.

We drove a fair way in fine weather to the trailhead, but the wind and rain returned as soon as we set out. I had, by this time, simply ceased to pay attention to the weather; it was too volatile to predict and whatever it was doing at the moment hardly mattered because, in ten minutes, it would be doing something else. To illustrate that point, within the hour—before we even reached the first shrine—the rain stopped and it became simply cloudy.

There are an astounding number of shrines in Ireland, at least in comparison to Clifton Park. This one was high up in the barren hills, but it was large and, by implication, important. We spent a few minutes inspecting it before continuing along the path, which was gratifyingly flat, firm and dry, most likely due to the hordes of pilgrims who had trudged their way to the shrine over the centuries.

Whatever the reason, I and my knee were glad for it. The smooth surface and gentle slopes meant my leg stayed in top form and made the walking—for the first time that week—almost pleasurable. The other hikes felt like forced marches compared to this pleasant stroll in the countryside and I believed the others felt that way, too. As we ambled along, we linked ourselves into pairs and trios, walking together temporarily while exchanging conversation, and then split up to reform with someone else. I hiked with Bob for a while, and learned more about his fascinating life, then joined up with Ros and Richard for a course in B&B management.

At some point, Siobhán and I drifted into each other's orbit and began to chat. We talked about our families, our childhoods, life in our respective countries and the differences in our cultures. We talked about books and movies and hikes we had been on and somehow, for the remainder of that morning, we never got around to drifting into a conversation with anyone else. When we stopped for lunch, we were still together, still talking. We ate our lunch sitting next to each other on a dry stone wall and continued talking.

It was a relief to feel comfortable and relaxed with someone and, although Siobhán was by far the most reticent and shy member of the group, she seemed comfortable and relaxed talking with me, as well, so after lunch, we continued on our way, still paired up and still talking. The weather remained agreeable, the ground remained firm and our feet remained dry; it seemed as if it was going to be a stunning day. Then Jon consulted his map and told us we were leaving the dirt track to follow the path around a distant lake to the rendezvous point with our van.

The path Jon pointed at was not a path as I knew them; the paths I walked were easily discernable and well-marked. Wherever you were on the trails I hiked, you could look ahead and see a marker affixed to a tree or a post, and if you turned around you would see another one marking where you had come from. Here, there was nothing but a desolate greenish-brown landscape undulating into the distance. At intervals far enough apart to make them nearly meaningless were trail markers, or at least that was what Jon referred to them as. To me, they looked like stakes some local farmers had put up randomly throughout the wastelands as a joke on us foreigners.

Whatever they were and however they got there, we left a perfectly dry and well-traveled path to follow them. Almost immediately, we sank up to our ankles. The ground was a soggy quagmire of weeds and the only way across was to skip from tuft to tuft. This made the going slow and my knee throb in an alarming manner.

For mile after mile we slogged through the marshlands, all of us aching, sore, wet and miserable. I was pleased to see that my companions were as disheartened by the terrain as I was, but when their grumbling reached Jon, he just shrugged.

"You have to take what the trail throws at you," was all he said.

Grumbling even louder, we continued on.

Siobhán was feeling the strain, and my knee made walking difficult. We ended up in the back, marching in the rear, chatting, telling jokes and singing songs to keep our spirits up. We made a good team; I carried her pack up the hills, she gave me pain medication and we kept each other laughing. We tried not to dwell on the fact that we were a long way from anywhere, and that if one of us sustained an injury (they all kept looking worryingly at my leg) it would be a hard job to get them out. The other unsettling fact was Jon and his insistence on sticking to trails he had never been on before; none of us—Jon included—truly knew where we were, where we were going or what we might stumble into along the way.

We were beginning our fifteenth refrain of *Climb Every Mountain* when, in the far distance, we saw the front segment of our group assembling on a bridge. This gave us hope; we were heading toward a road, dry land and a way out, but they were still a long way off and catching up with them was a slow and painful process. They looked dry and comfortable gathered, as they were, on sturdy boards held up by steel girders, but where we were, it was still wet and treacherous and our progress was measured in inches. We moved from tuft to tuft, keeping our eyes, and our hopes, on the distant bridge.

When we finally reached it, however, we met with more disappointment: the bridge was not a bridge passing over anything, or going from anywhere to someplace else, it was simply a bridge. It sat, inexplicably, in the middle of the marsh, for no discernable reason except to disappoint us. I decided it must have been built by the same farmers who had scattered the trail markers.

Still, it was dry and got us above the marsh for a few minutes. Siobhán and I arrived, on our eighty-seventh refrain of *Climb Every Mountain*, and were just on the "...fooooord every stream" part when Jon told us to shut up. Apparently, it was bad moods all round by then. Siobhán and I joked about being the bad kids in the back as Jon led us off the bridge and back in to the marsh.

From there, the day spiraled into a series of agonizing footsteps. It was the bog all over again; put one foot in front of the other, only it was much more difficult when hopping from tuft to tuft. The scenery, I was told, was spectacular, but I didn't dare lift my eyes to take it in; I had to keep a careful watch on my footing or I would end up in the swamp. The only relief during that long afternoon came in the form of a whispered message passed back from the front lines. Up ahead, we were told, Margaret had finally heard one too many banalities about taking what the trail throws at you from Jon and—while stranded on a tuft and unable to move without ending up knee-deep in the marsh—she loudly and vociferously told him where he could stuff his hike.

This gave us something to smile about as we grimly made our way forward.

At length we came to some firmer ground. It was still wet and treacherous, but it wasn't a swamp and we began making better time. Siobhán and I were still bringing up the rear, but we now had the company of several of the others who were equally fatigued and footsore.

With the end getting closer, our spirits and our pace picked up. Then, as we were coming off a small hill, Siobhán suddenly sank up to her thigh in a stray bog hole; one moment she was walking beside me, the next she was suddenly half my height. It was some job getting her out. I grasped her under the arms and pushed up with my good leg while she used her walking stick for leverage. Eventually, I returned her to firm ground, and noticed I was still holding her. I stepped away with a strange sense of regret, and let my hand linger, for a few brief moments, on her arm.

The ground became firmer after that, and eventually we found a dirt track that turned into a narrow road. As we approached the cusp of the civilized world, our bedraggled group passed a young boy and his father fishing in a small lake. The boy looked at us in wonder.

"Where did you come from?" he asked.

"About fourteen miles that way," Margaret said, pointing. Then she bent down to his level. "I thought the leprechauns were going to get us." The boy's father shook his head and turned back to his fishing pole. "Sure and no leprechaun would be mad enough to go walking back there," he said.

A little further on, the van that was waiting to pick us up at the end of the road drove in to get us. We were already two hours late and the driver didn't feel like waiting around any longer. None of us minded.

The van drove us to the hotel where, showered, medicated and wearing the second of my sons' three shirts, I joined the others for dinner. The group had been right about the hotel; it was, as they said, posh, but it was too far removed from the closest town of Oughterard for us to want to walk, so after dinner, Judith, Siobhán, Jean-Denis and Mireille, and myself rented a taxi. On the ride into town, Judith asked the driver if he could recommend a good, traditional pub.

"Oh, now, I don't drink a'tal, a'tal," he said, but he dropped us outside of an establishment that seemed a likely place to catch some authentic Irish flavor, then he refused to come back for us at the time we asked him to.

"Eleven o'clock won't be long enough if you're out for a pint," he said. "I'll come back for you at half eleven."

The main bar area was small, well-lit and filling rapidly. We managed to secure a table and get in a round of drinks, then we spent the next hour bitching about the hikes, and the fact that we were being led by a madman who didn't know where he was going, and how dangerous that was, and didn't we think the tour company would want to know about this and then, once we'd let off steam and had a pint or two, we forgot all about it.

Despite being small and crowded, the pub felt authentic enough; the other customers were, at least, locals and not tourists, and the interior had that weathered, well-used look I had first noticed at the Sheebeen. When the entertainment began, however, I started to wish I was back at Eamonn's Pub in Loudonville so I could hear some good Irish music.

The band, which was comprised of two people playing a banjo, an accordion and a penny whistle, sounded like a pair of enthusiastic amateurs auditioning for a job in an Irish themed pub in Disney World. And failing. It was the type of tinny, trippy Irish music that would have been laughed out of Eamonn's and banned at the Hibernian Hall. They played "The Battle of New Orleans"—that popular Irish ditty that became Irish simply because an Irishman sang it—and if I hadn't been familiar with the song I never would have recognized it. And I was sorry I had; they were ruining it for me.

The crowd remained indifferent, whereas I thought insulted would have been a more appropriate response. I supposed the locals were inured to the butchery of their national music, but it made me feel sad and slightly embarrassed. I couldn't express these observations to the group, however, because the band was employing the time-honored tradition of concealing lack of talent beneath a blanket of sound, and as soon as the cacophony began our conversation came to a halt. All I could do was sip my pint and wait for half eleven, whenever that might be.

Inishmore

The hotel was dark when we returned that evening, despite the fact that we were home before midnight. This was strange to me; I had never seen a hotel close down for the night. That's the sort of behavior I would expect from a B&B, but a hotel, if it's not going to wait up for its guests, it ought to at least leave a night light on.

There was a bell, and after leaning on it for about ten minutes, someone came to grudgingly unlock the front door and let us in. We went straight to our rooms—it wasn't as if we had the option of having a nightcap in the hotel bar—and after a truncated night's sleep, I woke to a sore knee and rising panic. This was, they assured me, a rest day. We were scheduled to tour the island of Inishmore and, in the afternoon, be transported to yet another hotel, which meant I would have no opportunity to seek out a Laundromat. I had only one of the souvenir shirts left, so I put on the one I had worn the night before—it was still fresh enough, and smelled only vaguely of tobacco smoke—along with the cleaner of my two pair of jeans.

Our luggage was once again going ahead without us—this time to a place called Lisdoonvarna—so I stuffed my dirty clothes and one clean shirt into the suitcase and bundled the remaining paraphernalia into the pack. They were both as full as they could get, but at least I was able to fit everything into them; it wasn't until they told us they were providing a packed lunch that the flaw in my plan became, yet again, painfully evident. With my back pack doubling as an auxiliary suitcase, I had nothing to carry my provisions, or anything else, in. I had just about resigned myself to making a hobo pack out of my jacket so I could carry the chicken sandwich, bag of chips and a bottle of apple juice around in it when Siobhán offered to let me put my lunch in her pack.

And so it was that we spent the day together.

We set off in the gray morning, taking a minibus to the pier then transferring, on foot, to the ferry for Inishmore, the largest of the Aran Islands. We sat together as a group on the trip over, taking in the sea air and enjoying the fact that we weren't slogging through a bog somewhere. When the ferry docked, the rest of the group all went their separate ways, leaving Siobhán and I to wander on our own.

I was, by this time, fairly certain Siobhán's name was not Siobhán. I'd heard her and Judith shouting at each other over the music the previous night and had caught a name that sounded like Sheena or, perhaps, Xena—she of Warrior Princess fame. Fortunately, I was not a huge fan of the series, and I happen to have a niece named Sheena, so I managed to trade Siobhán in for a new, possibly correct, name that did not have me conjuring up images of Lucy Lawless wearing a metal bodice and wielding a broadsword. Though, that's kind of a shame.

We spent the morning wandering around what there was of the island. It was beautiful in a bleak, Wuthering Heights sort of way, with ancient tombstones leaning drunkenly in desolate graveyards and brooding Celtic crosses scattered randomly over the barren and rocky landscape, but then the sky cleared and the sun came out, transforming the look from romantic gothic to simply desolate. We walked along the road that ran through the middle of the island until it became obvious the scenery wasn't going to change, then we turned around for a walk along the muddy beach on our way back to the pier and the sparse collection of tourist shops.

Being a woman, Sheena's method of shopping involved a lot of touching. The first thing she touched was a thick, knitted sweater with a Celtic design woven into the front. She felt the wool, ran her hand over the design, then picked up another sweater, and another as she worked her way through the small store. After she had touched the entire inventory of the shop, we left without buying anything and went to the next shop to repeat the process.

The sky had cleared and the sun was high so we sat on a stone wall to eat our lunch, looking out at the ocean and the stranded boats lying on their sides in the muddy bottom of the empty bay. After we finished, Sheena showed me how to crumple up the chip bag so that it became a tight little capsule. It was a trick she'd learned from the Ramblers, and it was a handy thing to know if you needed to keep your trash compact and neat. That was pretty much our entertainment for the day.

Having spent a few hours walking around, we decided to find a place to sit and have a drink. Our choices were limited, as there appeared to be only one bar on the island. Initially, it looked far from promising; it was housed in a cinderblock box that had been painted a sickly yellow at some point in the past and christened with the unlikely and uninviting name of "The Inis Mór American Bar." It looked like a biker bar or a down-at-heel social club, and the name inspired visions of flashing lights, disco balls and a bartender wearing a sequined vest embroidered with the name "Spike."

Happily, it was neither of those extremes, but simply a comfortable room with wooden benches, a few tables and an expansive bar with a young, dark-haired woman behind it. A few locals sat at the bar and in the corner two grizzled men chatted in Gaelic. They turned to look as we entered, but none of them gave us the "You're not from around here" stare we would have received if we had entered a strange bar in New York. We sat at a table and I went to the bar to order drinks.

Sheena's drink—a white wine spritzer—was thrown together without much thought, but I ordered a Guinness, and the fetching young lady responsible for drinks procurement evidently regarded Guinness pouring as a matter of pride. She drew the first two-thirds of the drink and allowed it to settle while I stood looking thirstily on. She then began the topping up process, which involved getting just the right amount of Guinness and foam to coalesce into the optimum Guinness-head thickness. She poured some, checked it with a level and a set of calipers, poured some more, checked again, and poured a bit more. By now Sheena was in need of another drink and I was thinking of maybe catching the ferry back to the mainland to buy a six pack of Coors to tide me over. There was no rushing this resident Picasso of the Guinness foam, however. She continued to pour and check with intense concentration, but her artistic frustration soon began to rise. She demonstrated this by unceremoniously dumping the full pint into the sink and starting over with a clean canvas, I mean, glass.

Sometime during the next hour I received what she obviously considered to be the perfect pint of Guinness (yet she hadn't even bothered to draw a shamrock in the foam). I felt I should take a photo of it, but instead I just drank it without even stopping to appreciate the uniformity of the foam and the artistic flair of the cascading bubbles or whatever the hell it was that she was after.

We sipped our drinks and continued talking, and it came to mind, once again, how enjoyable being with Sheena was; the conversation suffered no awkward lags or embarrassing pretentions that an actual date would occasion. I put this down to expectations: we had none.

There were, in fact, none to be had. We were free to talk and laugh without the worry of saying the wrong thing or the pressure of doing the right thing because, in two days' time, she would be back in England and I would be safely, and singly, on my way. Not feeling the need to impress or pretend was a huge relief; I could just be me, something I would never have considered if I'd had romantic inclinations.

After our drinks, we returned to the first of the village shops we had visited earlier to buy the first thing Sheena had looked at that morning, proving to my satisfaction that women the world over share a similar shopping gene. She called the sweater she bought a jumper, which brought to my mind the type of garment Sheena referred to as a pinafore. And so the conversation continued.

We returned to the docks and rejoined the group for the short ferry ride back to the mainland and the shorter van ride to our new hotel. It was still early so I seized the opportunity to go into town and attempt to locate a Laundromat. It was my final chance.

Town was a short walk away and my knee, although aching from a day of wandering around the island, seemed fit enough. There was one more hike to go and I really didn't want to miss it. However, it was 13 miles with a 1,400 foot ascent, and I wasn't sure my knee could take much more slogging through bogs. But if I opted out now, with my leg not feeling so bad, I would look like a slacker. I mulled over my hiking options and prayed for some overdue luck in the laundry department. The best outcome would be an open store where I could buy more shirts and maybe another pair of pants; that would better serve me at this point as I couldn't exactly run back to the hotel to get my washing if I did discover a Laundromat. Maybe I really should skip the hike and try my luck at finding washing facilities the next day. I was weighing the alternatives when I suddenly found myself face down on concrete.

Without warning, my knee had given way, leaving me sprawled on the sidewalk.

This, at least, decided the question for me. I would surely have to miss the next day's hike, and could use the time to get my laundry done. I picked myself up, tested my leg and limped gingerly back toward the hotel.

In my room I rubbed some anti-inflammatory cream on my knee, wrapped it in the ACE bandage and took some pain killers. Then I limped down to the bar to get a much-needed drink. The bar was empty. Totally. No patrons, no bartender. In fact, the entire hotel seemed to be deserted. I poked my head into the back room, looked behind the bar, up and down the hallway. No one. So I sat on a bar stool and brooded.

I was sick of Ireland, sick of the chronic inconvenience, sick of being continually bewildered, sick of the weather, sick of the wet, sick of the cold. I was three thousand miles from home, alone and, more to the point, without a drink. The only bright spot was that I didn't have a tattoo. Then Judith and Sheena came down and I started feeling better.

With the arrival of more people, a bartender miraculously appeared and I managed to get a Guinness. Things were definitely looking up, especially when Sheena sat beside me. I noticed she was wearing a skirt and looking quite pretty, but I kept these thoughts to myself; rumors were already starting to circulate about me and Sheena. It was one thing for the others to get ideas about us being a couple; I didn't want Sheena to think I believed it myself.

I was waiting for Jon so I could tell him my decision about the next day's hike but before he arrived, Sheena leaned over to me.

"Judith is worried about your knee," she said quietly. "She thinks maybe you shouldn't go on the hike tomorrow, and if you want to do something else, maybe I could not go and we could maybe spend the day together."

"I already decided not to go."

"Oh. Well, then…"

"But, if you want, we could still do something. I need to get my laundry done, but we could do something in the afternoon."

"It's just that Judith was worried, you see, and, well, sure, we could do something."

At this point, she leaned over and whispered to Judith. Judith nodded her approval, and beamed, looking so exceedingly pleased that I had to wonder if her self-congratulations were due to having convinced me to forgo the hike or for having successfully arranged to put Sheena and me together for the day.

When Jon arrived, I told him I was opting out of the final hike. Everyone in the room seemed relieved at my decision, no doubt thankful that they wouldn't have to take turns carrying me through the final nine miles of bogs if I had decided to go. Even Jon took the news well, seeming to accept that my malingering was for the greater good, though I still think he would have liked to have seen me court-martialed and shot.

When Sheena announced her defection, it occasioned an unsettling amount of approval from the rest of the group. After they turned their attention away from us, Sheena leaned toward me once more.

"They think we're sweet," she whispered.

I smiled conspiratorially at her and realized I liked the idea. Not of us being sweet on each other, but of the group thinking it—it just seemed right. And no matter what anyone thought, we knew the truth, and even though we weren't sweet, we would be spending the day together and I suddenly realized I was going to miss her when she returned to England.

The Cliffs of Moher

My knee felt fine the next morning. It seemed to be trying to fool me into going on the hike but, having betrayed me the previous afternoon, I wasn't about to change my plans based on its sudden, and clearly cynical, promise to behave itself.

All of the clothes in my suitcase were now officially too dirty to wear, especially if I was going to be with Sheena all day. I had only the final souvenir shirt, my last pair of underwear, a set of recycled socks and my emergency shorts to assemble into a clean outfit. Why I had brought the shorts, I couldn't imagine; I rarely wore shorts so I must have, in a moment of clarity, thrown them in with the rest of my wardrobe "just in case." Whatever the reason, it turned out to be one of the smarter things I did; if I did find a Laundromat, I could have both pairs of pants washed. If I didn't, of course, I would be dressing like a hobo for the rest of the trip.

Hikers, I found, are fond of shorts and some of our company wore them almost exclusively. Thus inured to the sight, my showing up for breakfast in a pair of LL Bean pleated front chino shorts and my fish-belly white legs elicited none of the pointing and laughing I otherwise would have expected. The day's march was plotted out over scrambled eggs, bacon and tea but Sheena and I remained aloof, caught up in our musing about what we were going to do with our free time.

94

When the rest of our crew departed for the hike, I returned to my room and packed all of my dirty clothes into my laundry bag. Then I went to the lobby to meet up with Sheena, wearing my jacket, short sleeved shirt and comedy shorts (on me, all shorts are comical) and carrying a sack full of dirty clothes. If I had been trying to impress her, this would have caused considerable embarrassment, but as we were simply temporary trail buddies, exposing my true—unorganized and not altogether suave—self caused no inkling of self-consciousness.

We decided to walk into town and hunt down a Laundromat; a brave choice, seeing as how I had not uncovered a sniff of one during the previous week. It was, however, our only option, aside from schlepping the laundry bag around with us for the remainder of the day, so we set off into the cool morning, with its low clouds and ever-present threat of rain.

In town, Sheena sought out a visitors' information center where she perused brochures advertizing local attractions while I—still clinging to the idea that Irish people must, on occasion, wash their clothing—asked the kind woman behind the counter for the location of a Laundromat. She was, as her job description indicated, full of information. She told me the address of a woman who took in laundry and recommended a visit to the Cliffs of Moher.

Back on the street, fine rain began to fall. We walked in the strengthening shower to the address the information lady had given us only to find out the laundry didn't open until ten o'clock, so the three of us—Sheena, me and the sack of laundry—wandered the lanes of Lisdoonvarna for a while, taking in what sights we could until the appointed hour. We returned to the laundry at ten and found it open and very accommodating. The Laundromat was actually the woman's home, but she relieved me of my bundle of dirty clothes, promising to have it clean, dry and folded by three in the afternoon. We weren't exactly sure when we would be getting back but she told me not to worry; if I couldn't pick up the laundry by six o'clock, she would leave it at the Royal Spa.

"They'll have it behind the bar," she assured me.

Unburdened, we went back to the main street, found a cab and had him take us to the Cliffs of Moher.

The cliffs, without a doubt, were the most stunning sight I had seen to date. The gentle, green land rolled languidly to the coast, giving no hint of drama, then, just before it reached the ocean, a layer of rock jutted from beneath the grass forming a shelf, as flat and wide as a promenade, before plunging 700 feet into the Atlantic Ocean. The cliffs cover a five mile section of the coast in a zigzag course, affording spectacular views of both the ocean and the cliffs themselves. At least that's what the brochure said. They certainly were an impressive sight, but this was not what I found most spectacular: the most amazing thing was the absence of any sort of fence, railing, roped boundary or other demarcation designed to keep people a safe distance from the edge. They didn't even have any signs warning people of the dangers inherent in getting too near a cliff edge. I thought back to the New York State government's attempt to fence off our local viewpoint and thanked whatever gods there were that the Irish did not feel the need to be reminded of the fact that falling off a cliff could be hazardous to your health. So while the view was undeniably magnificent, the most startling aspect of it—to my coddled American mind—was how unspoiled it was.

Sheena and I walked along the path, safely distanced from the edge, admiring the craggy cliff faces where they met the restless ocean in a swirl of spray and foam, and gaping at the other tourists who were wandering nonchalantly up to the precipice and gazing casually into certain death.

I admit to being a weenie where heights are concerned, but that is not because I am afraid of heights.

In fact, I love heights; I find heights thrilling, the views expansive, and the idea of falling petrifying. Although, come to think of it, I don't even mind the idea of falling; as a teenager, I spent my summer afternoons jumping from the cliffs in Stuyvesant Falls into the Kinderhook Creek. Free falling is exhilarating; I'm all for it. It's the sudden stop at the end that terrifies me. Consequently, we stayed on the path and regarded the daredevil tourists with utter disbelief.

Still, the lure of the drop drew me; I had to see what was over the edge. Sheena, to my relief, declined to join me—the last thing I need when I am terrified is someone else being terrified right next to me—and I set out, gingerly, toward the rim. Never mind that some people were strolling as if on a city sidewalk, and that others were actually sitting with their legs dangling over the precipice (that is wrong; so very, very wrong), I began crawling when I was twenty feet away. At fifteen feet, I was flat on my belly, inching forward, my camera clasped so tight in my hands that I was leaving thumbprints. Eventually I reached that place where the rock stopped and thin air abruptly began. The drop was amazingly sudden and sheer; in one place, you were on solid rock; one inch further on, if you didn't have wings, you were dead. I peered into the abyss, snapped a quick picture and scooted backwards, not trusting myself to stand until I was ten feet from the edge.

Safely on firm and level ground, we continued our stroll and our never-ending exploration of the differences in our cultures. We talked about our daily routines, childhood games we had played, nursery rhymes, holiday traditions, driving and getting a license. We were sitting on a rock, looking out at the ocean when this particular subject arose, and it quite naturally encouraged us to take out our respective driving licenses and compare them. As we remarked on the differences, I realized I had unwittingly been presented with the opportunity of finally seeing Sheena's name, correctly spelled out and verified by the Ministry of Automobile Licensing, or whatever they had over there. I looked at her name, then looked at it again; it was a combination of letters I had never seen before, would never have thought to put together in that order myself and one I was certain to mispronounce. Fortunately, she noticed my brow furrowing.

"Yes, that's an unusual spelling of the name, isn't it?"

I agreed it was.

"It's the Scottish spelling; I have my dad to thank for that."

I nodded and said nothing.

"Some people mispronounce it as, 'SHO-naguh.'"

As, indeed, would I.

I had given up all hope of ever knowing this woman's correct name when she, mercifully, continued.

"I have to keep reminding people that the 'gh' is silent, and it's just 'SHO na' without the 'guh' tacked on."

I gave her back her license. So it was "Shona" or "Shonagh" without the "guh."

"That's fascinating," I said, and meant it.

We resumed our walk then, ambling back toward the area that passed as a visitor center and then onto the path that followed the cliffs north. As we walked, the low clouds thinned and the sun broke through. By the time we reached the end of the cliffs—the logical point to turn around and head back to the visitor center—the day had become so pleasant that we kept walking.

We strolled along a coast road, with the now blue and tranquil ocean to our left, green rolling meadows to our right, and a clear sky arching overhead. We walked and talked and eventually saw, in the distance, the seaside village of Doolin. It lay nestled in a dip too shallow to be considered a valley, and spread along the edge of a curve in the coast too slight to be considered a cove. But it was a pretty sight, a scattering of predominantly yellow cottages interspersed with enough red, pink and gray ones to make it interesting but not overbearing. A single road—the one we were on—ran through the middle. It was a sleepy place, quiet and seemingly deserted, but there was a pub and we headed there to get some lunch.

The dimness of the pub contrasted sharply with the brightness of the day, but once my eyes adjusted I saw that this was where everyone was. This felt, to me, more genuine than the pub we had visited in Oughterard, or the forgettable pub Judith, Sheena—I mean, Shonagh—and I had visited the previous evening (so nondescript I hadn't even bothered to mention it in my journal) or even the Sheebeen, which, for all its rustic interior, had an underlying touristy feel to it. This was a real pub, filled with authentic people and serving authentic food, like steak and Guinness stew, which I had never before heard of but instantly proposed to try. We found a table and Shonagh ordered sea food while I sampled the stew. It was hot and meaty with the underlying, but not overpowering, flavor of Guinness, a culinary combination it would not have naturally occurred to me to attempt. It made me glad for the Irish who, in these rural parts of the island, obviously had a lot of time, and Guinness, on their hands.

From Doolin, we followed a road inland that we hoped would lead us to Lisdoonvarna. The sun was high in the sky and the day had become uncharacteristically hot. Our jackets were now packed away and there was nothing between the summer sun and my pasty-white arms, face and legs. At the time, I never gave it a thought; I was totally focused on Shonagh.

Contrary to the usual laws of relativity (perception of time shortens in direct proportion to the desirability of the company) the walk seemed to go on forever. The ease we felt in each other's company, coupled with the sudden return of summer weather, injected a feeling of benign languidness into the day, which we accepted without hesitation. While the others were, no doubt, route-marching through bogs and wetlands, we ambled, heeding no deadlines and little caring if we were on the right road or not.

With the coastline behind us, we found ourselves surrounded by pasture land, sheep and fresh-cut hayfields dotted with huge circular bales that resembled cheese wheels of the gods. Along the way, inspired by the scenery, we talked about hay-baling, and livestock, and how what farming methods we knew of were done. Then we talked about photography, knitting, music, comic books, road construction, gardening, aviation, shoes, chocolate, forestry, yoga, NATO, solar energy and cricket. I had never talked to any one person about so many inane subjects before, and yet I spent the afternoon in a state of utter fascination. It came to me, at some point, that if we had lived anywhere near one another, I would certainly make an attempt to see her again, so I counted myself lucky that she would be safely on a Sussex-bound jet the following afternoon.

Toward the end of the walk, our rambling conversation came round to our life stories again and, as Shonagh related how she had never married, I heard myself ask:

"Do you think you might ever want to get married some day?"

I stopped walking from shock, feeling as if I had unwittingly committed the verbal equivalent of sidling up to the edge of the Moher cliff and was now staring into the void. Shonagh stopped, too. She looked at the road and then at a distant field.

"I don't know," she said. "If the right bloke came along, I would definitely consider it."

Then she looked at me.

"And what about you?"

Panic struck. My mind locked. My mouth opened but no sound came out, as if my brain no longer trusted my voice to not betray me. Eventually, my vocal chords were let off with a warning.

"No, no, never," I said. "I was married and then I lived with a woman for eight years and neither relationship worked out." My hands took on a life of their own, ardently punctuating my words as if my voice alone was incapable of stressing my position stridently enough. "I'm through with women; I'm simply not cut out for long-term commitment."

Shocked by my own vehemence, I began walking again, and Shonagh fell silently into step beside me. As I mentally eased away from the cliff edge, I struggled to comprehend, not where the panic had come from, but how I had allowed myself to stride headlong into such dangerous territory. Slowly, my panic subsided and I glanced at Shonagh; she was studying the road, and I swear she was smirking.

Soon, we eased into safer topics and before long we were chatting happily, with the unfortunate incident behind us and, I hoped, forgotten.

By the time we reached the hotel it was late in the afternoon. Shonagh went to her room to change for dinner and, since I didn't have anything to change into, I went into town to retrieve my laundry. It was after six o'clock so I assumed the laundress was sitting down with a well-deserved Guinness after a hard day of washing and ironing, and went instead to the Royal Spa. I had never picked up my laundry from a bar before but the bartender didn't seem to think it strange. I told her who I was and she handed over my laundry sack, now filled with clean, pressed and neatly folded clothing. The custom, when picking up laundry from a pub, was to have a celebratory pint (I'd made this custom up that very moment) but the dinner hour was looming so, with regret, I and my laundry returned to the hotel.

While walking to and from town I became aware that I had caught some sun, but it wasn't until I dressed for dinner that I began to appreciate the full effects of ambling along a country road for several hours on a hot summer day. The sunburn on the back of my neck and arms was annoying, but something I was used to. The backs of my legs, however—which never see the light of day—felt like they had been flayed with a hot pumice stone. When I tried to walk, the coarse denim of my jeans rubbed the tender skin into fresh peaks of pain and I had to practice in my room until I could move without looking like a constipated robot.

At dinner, Shonagh and I sat on opposite ends of the table. I supposed that spending the day together had been enough for both of us and, if we had sat together at dinner, the rest of the company would jump to the natural, though incorrect, conclusion. This was to be our final dinner together, so there was a fair bit of reminiscing and the obligatory planning out of the next day's events. I was glad for the diversion; everyone seemed to have forgotten that they had Shonagh and I paired up, but then, after dinner was over, Judith invited us to accompany her into town for another try.

The three of us had gone to town the previous evening in search of a traditional Irish pub but ended up at a hideously American-looking bar with an equally hideous band. It had been an early night. This night was our final chance, however, so Judith wanted to make the most of it, or so she indicated.

We wandered the streets looking for the Ireland of our imagination but, being a Friday, most of the pubs were full and raucous. We finally found a bar with a halfway decent band playing halfway decent Irish folk-rock and elbowed our way in. Judith commandeered two seats at the bar but refused to accept my offer to stand so she could sit. Judith then bought a round, or, more specifically, she bought a drink for Shonagh and me. Then she disappeared.

When she didn't reappear, I waited for a lull in the music and shouted into Shonagh's ear.

"Where's Judith?"

"I think she left," she shouted in return.

"What for?"

"I think she wanted us to be alone so we could talk."

The band started up again, this time with a bagpiper. We left our drinks half-finished and walked the streets in blessed silence. We didn't talk much on our way back to the hotel; I suppose we felt we had said enough during the long, loquacious afternoon. I wondered, too, if Shonagh wasn't feeling a bit like me— sad that this would be our last walk together, glad for the times we had shared and thankful that we hadn't further explored our feelings for each other. That would have been a mistake, an exercise that could have only led to grief and protracted, gooey goodbyes at the airport in the morning.

The fact of her imminent departure was a relief; in a few hours I could return to my cosseted single life, and she to hers. And if I felt an overpowering urge to hold her hand, what did that mean beyond an expression of gratitude for her friendship and company? I never got the chance to find out; earlier in the day she had walked with her hands languidly at her sides, but she now kept her arms folded across her chest, confirming to my mind that she was withdrawing into herself for the sake of our mutual emotional safety. Or maybe she was just cold.

When we arrived at the hotel, I walked her to her room, not as a romantic gesture or an attempt to draw out our time together, but simply because our rooms happened to be across the hall from each other.

"Good night," I said as we reached our doors.

"Good night."

There was no longing or sadness or expectation in her voice, just a clear, unencumbered valediction. But

as I turned away she leaned close, gave me a quick kiss
on the cheek and disappeared into her room.

The Charm of Lisdoonvarna

In later years I learned that Lisdoonvarna is the matchmaking capital of Ireland and has been for about 150 years. They were, in fact, getting ready to host about 40,000 hopeful singles who swoop into town every September for what is billed as the largest singles event in Europe. Most of the hopefuls end up pairing with one another, as the locals are all pretty well picked over by now—the town, at that time, had a population of just over 1,000—but the fact remains that Lisdoonvarna has a certain magic about it, a magic that causes people to fall in love. Now, I don't particularly believe in magic, but it would explain a lot.

Though Shonagh had been aloof on the walk back from the pub, she wasn't feeling that way when we reached the hotel. But what did that mean, really? We already knew we were fond of each other, so nothing good could come from giving voice to those feelings. Perhaps the kiss was the culmination, the period (or "full stop," as Shonagh would say) to mark the end of our time together. To imbue it with any more meaning than that would be ridiculous, impractical and dangerous.

Sleep was a long time coming, and I woke to my travel alarm, which was a very unusual thing for me to do. I am usually awake early and use the alarm only as a back-up, but on that morning I seemed content to stay in bed, hording my dreams and delaying the moment when I would have to return to conscious thought. Our time together would be short, but it was a potential minefield. How could I keep a respectful distance yet not give her the idea that I was glad to be rid of her? And how would she react? Perhaps I could re-book the room, stay in bed and avoid the whole thing. I was not, after all, obligated to travel to the airport with them; I wasn't going home until Tuesday.

In the end, my responsible self won out. Pushing my protective self and worrisome thoughts aside, I took a shower—where I became startlingly reacquainted with my sunburn—packed and went down to breakfast. The day was beginning as the previous one had ended, with clear blue skies, a gentle breeze and a warm sun. While waiting for breakfast, I sat on the steps in front of the hotel, enjoying the unaccountably mild weather and projecting myself into the next few days.

Grateful as I was for my time spent hiking and my friendship with Shonagh, I had still not found what I had come to Ireland for: a glimpse of the real Ireland and the life-changing epiphany I felt destined to discover. Ireland wasn't a big place, but epiphanies are small and it could be hiding anywhere. I decided to go to Galway for no other reason than that was the name I chose to adopt during my Irish folk-singing days. As a singer, I went by the name of "Merv" and, after a while, people began to think that was my real name, a misconception I made no effort to disabuse them of. The reason for this mild deception had nothing to do with hiding from the tax man, Law officers or jealous husbands; it was simply convenient due to there being so many other people around named "Michael." The only time it became awkward was when someone insisted on knowing my last name.

I was singing in an Irish bar on St. Patrick's Day when it first happened and I judged that the raucous group querying me—a table full of O'Rileys, O'Connors and O'Dells—would cease being the agreeable audience they were if I told them I wasn't really Irish and was, in fact, descended from a long line of Lancashire Protestants. So I grasped for the first Irish-sounding word I could and told them my name was "Merv Galway." They liked that; instead of hounding me off the stage, they bought me a Guinness.

In American terms, Galway isn't far from Lisdoonvarna. Returning to Shannon airport with the group meant traveling further away, which seemed counterproductive, but the airport would be the best place to attempt to rent a car, as my trip to Westport had illustrated, and the bus ride offered the possibility of some more time with Shonagh, if she chose to sit with me.

While I was thinking that, she joined me on the step and sat next to me in the sunshine. It was strange how comfortable and natural it felt having her beside me. We fell into our easy rhythm of conversation, but it felt stilted, weighed down by the prospect of parting. When the opportunity arose, I presented her with the Claddagh necklace I had bought as a token of our friendship. She accepted it with only mild shock and surprise. Then she leaned over and kissed my cheek again. She didn't disappear this time, but stayed with me, telling me how glad she was to have met me, and how I had made what could have been a really miserable holiday into something very special.

When we went in to eat, we once again sat at opposite ends of the table, our tacit method of informing the others, and confirming to ourselves, that nothing was going on between us. When breakfast ended, Jon told us we had an hour or so until the bus left and said we could do as we wished with it. I decided to go for a walk and asked Shonagh if she would like to come along. I fully expected her to decline on the pretext of having something urgent to attend to in her room, but instead she said, "Yes."

We left the hotel and found an idyllic little lane bordered by wildflowers and flitting butterflies. We wandered along it, under blue sky and sunshine, a moment so perfect it felt like a Disney movie. Unlike the previous evening, she did not walk with her arms crossed and, without meaning to, I took her hand; it seemed the natural thing to do. Her fingers entwined with mine and we continued along the lane. At length we came to a stone bridge, moss-covered, dappled with shade and spanning a babbling brook. There we paused. She sat on the bridge wall and I stood in front of her; we held hands and gazed into each other's eyes and I saw myself back at the Cliffs of Moher, careening toward the precipice, not in terror, but filled with an eager abandon that terrified me even more. When the cliff edge came in sight, when there was nothing before me but free, open ocean, I leapt willingly into the abyss.

Our lips met. Her arms encircled me as mine encircled her and I felt the warmth of her body and the exhilarating feeling that I was flying and had not crashed to the rocks below. Still, in the back of my mind, those few rational thoughts, unsullied by the soporific effects of infatuation, were running in circles and screaming, "Damage control! Damage control!"

I suppose, even as we left the bridge and walked back toward the hotel, even after we had spoken the unspeakable and confessed our feelings for each other, it still wasn't too late. We were both conscious of the fact that we would soon be heading to separate continents, so what future could there be? If I remained cautious, I still had a chance, but I was too giddy to be cautious. With our hands clasped and goofy grins on our faces, we returned to the bus and made everyone's day.

On the bus ride to Shannon, we sat together.

Along the way, we stopped at Ennis, the county town of Claire, where we were released for an hour or two of sightseeing and lunching before continuing on to Shannon and the afternoon flight that would take the bulk of the group back to England. Shonagh and I wandered off by ourselves and explored the town only until we found a park bench. Then we sat and talked the time away.

Oddly, we didn't talk about us, or our possible future, or what we might be heading into; we just talked. There was no conscious effort on either of our parts to eschew those subjects; it simply seemed more expedient to concentrate on enjoying our last few minutes together with comfortable conversation than an angst-ridden dialogue. So we sat, and held hands, and kissed, and talked in the easy, familiar manner I knew I was going to miss. Somehow, the impending flight melted from our minds; for those few minutes, the future did not exist and we concerned ourselves only with the now.

We never got around to eating lunch.

At the airport, I helped her carry her bags and stayed with her while she checked in. We then went to the Bureau de Change where she exchanged her Irish money for British pounds. We had compared money during one of our earlier talks, but I still found myself mesmerized by the pound coin—its dull, gold color, its heft, its thickness, its strange symbols and, to my American eyes, its overall exotic nature—so I asked if I might have one as a token to remember her by. It seemed a safe memento. Like the necklace, it did not imply any sort of commitment; it was just a coin, not a territorial marker. I slipped it into my pocket and we moved on to the car rental booths.

The shock I had experienced in Westport when the rental agency told me they were out of cars was mild compared to the shock of discovering the rental agency at the airport was similarly bereft of automobiles. I had never heard, nor could even conceive of such a thing. Then I went to the next counter and received the same answer. The third, fourth and fifth car rental agencies also had no cars to offer and I eventually resigned myself to bus travel.

"But there's still one more left," Shonagh said.

I looked at the final car rental agency, in a neglected booth at the end of the row—clearly the poor cousin of car rental agencies with a name overshadowed and made instantly forgettable by the Avis, Hertz and Enterprise signs.

"What's the use?" I said. "It's just a crappy little outfit, and if no one else has any cars, they certainly won't either."

"Well, it won't hurt to ask."

The exchange struck me as uncomfortably domestic, but I couldn't deny the logic of it so I tucked away my misgivings and asked the lady at the counter if she had any vehicles to rent.

And, of course, she did. One. A red Fiat Punto; a make of car I had never heard of. It was, however, an appropriate model—a compact four-door with a hatchback, big enough for my luggage yet small enough to fit on the narrow Irish roads. Bizarrely, although I only needed the car for three days, I ended up renting it for five because the five-day deal was cheaper. Still, it was more than I had thought it would (or should) be. Then they started piling daily insurance fees on top of that. I had the option of refusing but, seeing as how I was about to attempt driving on the wrong side of the road, I thought being insured up to the hilt might not be a bad idea. I drew the line at the Full Tank Waiver, which would allow me, for a fee, to bring the car back without a full tank. Without paying this extra fee, I would have to bring the car back with a full tank or face a penalty. It seemed a no-brainer; pay yet another fee, or simply fill up the tank on the way into the airport. I declined. It was a small victory, but I relished it nonetheless. After signing and initialing a multitude of documents and handing over large sums of money, I was suddenly mobile.

Shonagh and I went to the lot to appraise my new acquisition. It was a cute little car that would get good mileage and provide me with ample storage space. I put my carry-on case into the back and my pack on the passenger's seat and we were suddenly out of things to do. I offered to remain at the airport until the flight arrived but she declined, saying it would be boring and sad. I accepted the wisdom of this and together we faced the fact that our time was drawing swiftly to an end.

We went back to the terminal where I said my farewells to the rest of the group, some of whom insisted—if I happened to be in their neighborhood—that I drop by for a visit. The invitation was always directed to Shonagh and I as a couple, a status the group had been quick to solidify. Then we returned to the Punto to say goodbye for the last time.

Even at this point, I retained faint hopes of getting away from this encounter lumbered with nothing heavier than memories and a soft longing. Obligation was not the thought foremost in my mind when—in that moment of our final parting—I recalled my ill-advised notion of getting a tattoo. This occasion, sweet though it was, did not merit scarring my body for life, but it might be a good excuse for the consolation prize.

"A ring," I said. "A Claddagh ring; I finally have a reason to get one."

Instead of commenting, she pulled the silver and turquoise ring off her middle finger and placed it in my hand.

"Will this fit?" she asked.

I slipped it onto my right ring finger; it fit perfectly.

I kissed her, and asked, "So, am I your boyfriend?"

"If you want to be," she said.

"I do," I told her, "and you're my English girlfriend."

We kissed one last time and then she left. I watched until she disappeared from sight, conscious of the pound coin in my pocket, the unfamiliar heft of her ring on my finger and the slow panic creeping up my throat and threatening to strangle me.

Part II
Searching for Ireland

Galway Bound

The fact that they drove on the left in Ireland had not escaped my notice; I was very aware of it, I just didn't consider it an issue. And for the most part, it wasn't, at least on the wide, interstate-type roads I started out on. Leaving Shannon airport turned out to be no more difficult than leaving Newark airport, which is to say you need to pay attention and make quick decisions. Add to this the operation of a car from what I considered the passenger's seat on the mirror image of a freeway and you have a situation that requires all of your concentration. This turned out to be a good thing, as it kept me from banging my forehead on the steering wheel while screaming, "Stupid! Stupid! Stupid!"

What had I done to my life?

I tried to answer that question, or at least make sense of it, but an exit came up with the name of a town I didn't recognize on it, so the question, "Should I get off here or wait for a better offer?" took precedence. Eventually, I saw a sign for Ennis and, as that was sort of between Shannon and Galway, I headed in that direction.

The roads, I soon discovered, weren't like American roads. Oh, they were flat, came with a variety of lanes and were wide enough to accommodate a car, but they weren't very well signposted, and they were infected with this thing called a roundabout.

I was no stranger to roundabouts, or traffic circles, as they are known in New England, but in America the routes are properly and clearly labeled so you know what direction to go in. Here, I was at the mercy of my irrational and irrevocable tendency to always take the first exit, which meant I was soon permanently, and for no reason other than the fact that I could not help myself, turning left.

This allowed me to tour a number of industrial complexes and squander an inordinate amount of time circling through the labyrinth of lanes in residential developments. It also caused me to pay full attention to what I was doing, leaving me no opportunity to analyze the question I had originally posed to myself about my life, what I had done to it and how, in the matter of a few short hours, I had managed to so thoroughly sabotage my hard-won and vigilantly guarded single status.

Hadn't the dark years with She-Who-Must-Not-Be-Named taught me anything? It might start out with the sweet feeling I could still feel glowing inside me, but it had a nasty habit of deteriorating into something ugly and sinister and difficult to untangle. The most abiding lesson I had taken with me when I finally extricated myself from She-Who-Must-Not-Be-Named was that freedom was sweet; sweet and precious and not something to be thrown away for a woman I had not yet gone shopping for a bottle of ketchup with; a woman who, despite our long and enjoyable conversations, I hardly even knew, even if she did sound like a BBC newsreader.

With more roundabouts coming up, there was nothing to be gained from dwelling on such thoughts, so I laid the question to rest, shoving it into the mental equivalent of my sock-drawer where it continued to poke its head up and harass me but, thankfully, left enough of my brain functioning to allow me to drive in the direction I was pretty sure might lead me to Galway.

I had no way of knowing what I would find when and if I arrived; Galway promised to be a city-type place—judging from its size on the map—so there should be lodgings, pubs, restaurants and, most importantly, Irish people doing Irish-type things. It seemed a good plan and I am certain it would have worked if:

- They put meaningful signs along the roads
- The car stopped turning left at every roundabout
- My knee hadn't started complaining
- I wasn't sitting in an oven disguised as a Punto

Being lost is a condition I am familiar with, so that wasn't a problem. However, being lost in a strange country—where the English words on the intermittent road signs are no less indecipherable than the Gaelic phrases that accompany them—was. Occasionally, I would see a sign saying something like, "Orgagort 2 miles," and, a mile later, another sign reading, "Orgagort 5 miles," indicating Orgagort had somehow shifted during the previous two or three minutes. This meant that, not only was I unable to comprehend the signs, if I did managed to find one I could read, I wouldn't be able to trust it.

And so I drove at random, searching for clues, kept alert by the stabbing pain in my knee every time I stepped on the clutch, and becoming intensely interested in the cage match my denim jeans and sunburned legs were apparently engaged in. The jeans were clearly winning, as the sunburn was getting really, really angry, and the heat wasn't helping at all.

Although it was late in the afternoon the sun was still high and hot, maintaining the heat that had built up in the car over the morning hours while it sat patiently in the airport lot, like a trapdoor spider, waiting for an unsuspecting customer to drag inside its hell-hole interior. The car, naturally, had no air conditioning, but it also had windows that did not open. I searched in vain for a handle so I could crank the window down, but found none. There were window cranks on the back doors, but not on the front. In my spare moments between turning left, scanning the roadsides for signs and grimacing in pain, I undertook a diligent study of the driver's door, pressing, poking, prodding and twisting everything that was pressable, pokable, prodable or twistable in the hopes that it might make the window go down. Nothing worked, so I accepted the fact that Irish cars were prohibited by law from having their front windows rolled down. I could think of no logical reason for a law like this, but current circumstances left me no choice but to accept it.

The result of these combined driving handicaps meant that I ended up near Ennis about the time I had expected to be in Galway. Feeling I had toured enough industrial complexes and seen my share of housing developments, I elected to stop. The only problem with that idea was that the streets were lined with plastic cones making parking impossible. Also, all of the hotels, motels and B&Bs I passed had their No Vacancy signs displayed. I was considering pressing on to Galway when I saw a restaurant/pub/motel combo with a parking lot and no sign—Vacancy or otherwise—anywhere in sight. Surrendering more to fatigue than hope, I pulled into the lot and parked.

Getting out of the car was agony, so I put that off for a while and simply opened the door to allow some relatively cooler air to waft into the interior. After manually hauling my leg out of the car and standing up on it, the pain began to abate and I was able to walk into the motel office. It was a tiny space, featuring a desk, a rack of tourist brochures and nothing else, not even a bell to summon the absent desk clerk, so I returned to the parking lot to have a look around. The motel sat on the edge of Ennis inside of a large paved patch of ground bordered by roads. It was an area with definite delineations, but generous enough to allow room to sprawl. From my side, I saw what looked like a row of attached sheds painted a color that landed somewhere between red and orange that I assumed to be the rooms. A sign hanging on the wall outside of the office door promised a pub and restaurant on the premises, so I went searching for them.

The restaurant was behind the rooms, facing another parking lot. The lot was half full, but the restaurant was empty, and so was the pub, save for a lone man working behind the bar who turned out to be, not only the bartender, but the motel clerk, bell captain and maître d' as well. When I told him what I wanted he led me through a maze of narrow hallways to an empty motel room; it boasted no frills, but it was clean and would suit me well enough. Tired and aching as I was, it would have had to have been a corner of hell to make me consider turning it down. I told him I'd take it. He accepted my answer with a jovial handshake and began to walk away.

"What time is check out?" I asked.

"Well, when do you want to check out?" he said. "We don't rush people out. When would you be wanting breakfast?"

"About eight o'clock."

He nodded.

"The staff arrives about eight so that should be fine."

He then went on to inform me about a hurling tournament in town—which was why almost everyone was booked up, and explained all those traffic cones in the streets.

"Leave your car here and walk into town," he advised. "It's a ten minute walk and such a fine day."

I thanked him and he left. I had just begun my unpacking routine when he returned.

"Could I have a name?" he asked.

I told him, then asked, "Could I have a price?"

He shrugged. "Oh, twenty five, thirty, whatever you can take."

We left it at that, figuring we could negotiate a price in the morning, and he left me to get on with my unpacking. He obviously wasn't going to charge a lot for the room and I obviously wasn't going to run off without paying, not now that he had my name. Still, it wasn't the sort of attitude one would expect to find in America; perhaps I might discover the real Ireland after all.

After performing a minimum of unpacking—to lessen the chance of me leaving something behind again—I headed into town. It was just after six o'clock, and turning into a lovely evening. I had expected to find the streets deserted, as usual, but I found an unusually large number of people out and about. Also unusual was the fact that they all seemed to be in a hurry. Unsure of myself as always, I asked someone how to get to the main street in town and he barely stopped as he pointed the way. An Irishman not wanting to stop and talk; there was clearly something strange going on.

Nearer to town, I noticed that the people were all heading in the same direction, so I fell into step with them and allowed myself to be carried with the crowd. Soon, I found we were heading for a stadium and saw a sign reading, "The All-Ireland U21 Hurling Semi-Finals: Galway (Gaillimh) vs Limerick (Luimneach)." I let the crowd lead me into the stadium where I paid my five pound entrance fee and went up into the stands.

It was then that I discovered why they call them "stands." It wasn't a misnomer; I was actually expected to stand on raised concrete steps, along with the thousands of other spectators. It was odd not having a seat I could claim as my own, so I crowded onto the platform with everyone else and staked out a bit of concrete, gripping the railing in front of me to show that this was my territory. As the incoming crowds filled up the stadium, we waited for the action to begin.

The game kicked off with a national anthem. At least that's what I assumed it was; I couldn't actually understand the words but the crowd sang with gusto and then began to roar, waving team flags and beating drums as the players came onto the field.

That was the height of the excitement for me, as the game itself turned out to be an unfathomable mix of lacrosse, baseball, football, soccer and a barroom brawl. I watched in bewildered amazement as those around me cheered and shouted encouragements ("C'mon lads!") and when I felt I had gotten my five pounds worth, I slipped away and went into town.

Now the streets *were* deserted, because everyone was at the game.

I found a genial, though practically empty, pub and enjoyed a leisurely meal of fish and chips. The solitude encouraged my thoughts to stray back to Shonagh, so after dinner, I returned to the deserted streets to have a look around. It occurred to me that, once the game ended, the town would be flooded with excited people— either of the jovial or angry variety—which would bring a whole new flavor to my environment. Soon, I heard them coming, and as they didn't seem to be turning over cars and setting fire to buildings as they approached, I assumed their team had won. In a short time, the streets were heaving and the pubs were full. I squeezed inside the next one I came to, elbowed my way to the bar to order a Guinness and then found a seat on a stool next to the wall where I watched the heretofore pleasant evening disintegrate.

The young men in the bar were dressed in the same slovenly manner as young men in the bars back home would be and they were drinking, heaven help me, Budweiser from long-neck bottles while WWF wrestling droned on in the background from the multiple televisions. There was no Irishness anywhere; even the buzz of their conversations sounded the same as any I would hear in the States. If I had been plunked down in the middle of the bar, I would have no way of knowing I was not in America. Then the music picked up loud enough for me to hear; it was all American pop songs, and when "Eternal Flame" by the Bangles came on I began to feel maudlin and very, very lonely, so I left.

Killarney

I slept poorly that night, waking in the darkness confused and disoriented, filled with a disquieting sense of elation mixed with terror; feelings that would not go quietly back into the sock drawer. These feelings merited, nay demanded, contemplation, but this was neither the time nor place. In order to sift logically through my emotions, inspect the ramifications of my declaration and more accurately judge the size of the obstacles I had willingly accepted, I needed to be in familiar surroundings, in a place where I could at least be certain of my base mindset. And Ireland was not that place, so with sleep escaping me, I rose early, packed carefully and waited in the dim morning for breakfast.

After the sun rose and I was fed and caffeinated and on the road again, I felt much better; pending adventure and present adversity kept my mind focused and my panic at bay. It was another sunny day, promising to be even hotter than the previous one, and already the car was stifling. I had still not figured out how to roll the front window down, so I rolled one of the back ones down, instead. However, this caused the air pressure in the car to WHUMP, WHUMP, WHUMP painfully against my eardrums so I had to stop and roll it up.

My goal was still Galway so, after consulting the map, I set out on the road I thought was sure to take me there. It didn't take long to become hopelessly lost. I didn't agonize about it—Ireland is a relatively small place so I figured I should come upon something recognizable sooner or later. As it was, however, I kept passing through villages with narrow streets and no names (or, at least, names that appeared on my map), then I would turn left at the roundabout and tour the local industrial complex or find myself on a major highway going, I hoped, in the right direction.

Driving on the left didn't give me as many problems on that second day, the only difficultly being an incomplete grasp of the fact that, in driving on the left, I was on the right side of the car so most of the car was to the left of me, not to the right. I became reminded of this when, on several occasions, I ran into roadside bushes. In one village, while negotiating a narrow street with a high, stone wall bordering the road, I heard a slight "thunk" and then noticed my passenger side wing mirror knocked up against the door frame. After that, I made a point of continually reminding myself to keep more to the middle of the road.

Otherwise, as long as there were cars on the roads, I didn't have much of a problem, but if I turned onto an empty road—lacking in any vehicular visual clues—I would "go American" and begin driving on the right again. As I was, at this point, somewhere in rural Ireland, I could go quite a ways before encountering another vehicle. It was always interesting to see it approaching from some distance away and then become slowly aware that we were heading directly toward each other, which was followed by a moment of bewilderment, wondering why the car was on the wrong side of the road before finally figuring out it was me.

In this way, I passed an exciting morning, but as noon approached and Galway did not appear, I had to assume I was not actually headed in the right direction. In fact after a few hours had passed, I entered the town of Tralee, which I recognized thanks to the famous rose that comes from there—and if I was not familiar with that fact, the giant banner spanning the main street

122

would have served as a reminder. What I was not aware of was where, precisely, Tralee was in relation to Galway, the answer being three counties and over 100 miles south. Had I known that, it wouldn't have bothered me a great deal; I had tacitly given up on the idea of getting to Galway after about the first hour. What did bother me was that, after Tralee—where I did not fancy stopping—no other cities, or even big towns, appeared. Although I was on vacation and not adhering to a schedule and not opposed to surprises, I still needed a destination.

At one point, sometime during the mid-afternoon, I found myself driving along the shore of a large lake. Since I was unable to ascertain my whereabouts, I pulled off the road to see if I could locate the lake—and thereby my own general location—on the map. It was a big lake; huge, in fact, so I was surprised when I couldn't match it up with any features showing on my map. Eventually, a local walking his dog passed by so I pointed to the water and called to him.

"Could you tell me the name of that lake?"

The man looked at me quizzically.

"It's the Atlantic Ocean," he said, and sauntered on.

Back in the car, I headed inland. By now I was hot, tired, hungry and thirsty and, as far as I could tell, no closer to a destination. To add to my rising discomfort, the hours in the car had my knee in such a state that I had to physically lift my leg with my hands and manually push it down on the clutch pedal when changing gears, so finding a destination was becoming a matter of some urgency. Then I saw a young man hitchhiking. He seemed innocuous enough and, since he wasn't wearing a backpack or holding a cardboard sign reading, "Budapest," I figured he might have some local knowledge, so I stopped and picked him up.

"Where ya' heading?" I asked.

"Killarney."

"Is that far?"

"Not really."

And so I went to Killarney, where, as the song has it, the Devil is buried. As a bonus, the young man was on his way to visit his girlfriend and he was meeting her at a hotel just outside of town. The Killarney Court Hotel, he advised, would be a good place to stay if I was looking for lodging: it was convenient to the town, had modern, spacious rooms and a "car park" (a term which conjured up in my mind images of cars taking turns on the swings, clambering over the monkey bars and engaging in impromptu games of touch football). And best of all, he could guide me there. Based on that, I decided I would check in before I even saw the place.

With my destination decided upon for me, there was just one more mystery I needed clearing up.

"What is it about Irish cars?" I asked. "Why aren't you allowed to roll the front windows down? I've been riding around in this car for two days sweltering in the heat because it's impossible to get any air in here."

Without a word he leaned over and pushed a button on the dashboard. His window hummed and opened, letting in the fresh, cool breeze. There was really little to say after that; I just drove on, following his directions and watching as the scenery changed from merely hilly to the soft edge of rugged.

The hitchhiker did not steer me wrong, direction-wise or accommodation-wise. It occurred to me, as we pulled into the spacious parking lot and I gratefully turned off the engine, that he might have talked up the hotel to gain points with his girlfriend, who worked there, but it was all he promised, and more. Compared to some of the places I had been staying in, The Killarney Court bordered on elegance. The cost reflected that, but these were my last two nights in Ireland so I decided to splash out.

The room was large, comfortable and accommodating. I unpacked and prepared for the evening. The hitchhiker (no, I never did ask his name) had instructed me on how to get into town and what parts to avoid and other handy things a clueless American who couldn't figure out how to lower the windows in a car might need to know to keep himself out of trouble. When I returned to the lobby it was still fairly early but, since I hadn't eaten since breakfast, I decided to have an early dinner in the hotel restaurant before heading into town.

I allowed myself to be seated before taking a good look around, and it was only then that I noticed, from my solitary table for four, that I was nearly the only diner in the cavernous room. And it wasn't a fast-food restaurant or a pub where having dinner on your own was the norm. This was a place with linen table cloths, crystal wine glasses and centerpieces on the tables. It was the sort of place you would take your wife or girlfriend or, indeed, a woman you had just met who you had strong feelings for.

The food was superb but it couldn't mitigate how alone and far from home I felt. By the time I finished my meal I felt lonesome, homesick and in need of talking to someone, anyone. Well, maybe not just anyone. Shonagh, actually. And as I walked through the lobby on my way to the door, I saw a bank of phones and decided to do just that.

The episode with the phone that first morning in the B&B made me brave and it took less than half an hour to figure out how the phones worked, how to dial long distance and how to convince directory assistance to give me the phone number. I wasn't sure if it was a good idea or not and, had I thought about it, I would have probably decided it was a bad idea. So I didn't think about it; all I knew was I wanted to hear her voice. So I dialed. Incredibly, I heard the buzz of a ringing phone, and then a woman answered.

"Hello?"

"Hi," I said. "Can I speak with Shonagh?"

"This is she."

The voice sounded formal, almost matronly, like an elderly librarian. I thought perhaps I was talking to her mother, or a spinster aunt who happened to have the same name. I managed to resist asking, "Are you *sure* you're Shonagh?" and instead asked if maybe there was someone else at the address named Shonagh.

The woman sighed as if slightly exasperated.

"Michael," she said, in the non-librarian voice I recognized. "It's me."

The conversation went uphill from there, but only marginally. It was an awkward situation; I was still on the holiday she had already put behind her and she was back in her normal life, and connecting our disparate worlds via a courtesy phone in the lobby of a hotel made me feel very self-conscious. She told me I had caught her in the middle of dinner, so I let her go.

For me, the phone call was achingly disappointing; I had hoped to get some clear indication that her feelings for me had not evaporated as soon as she touched familiar ground. While she never gave any indication that they had, she gave no indications to the contrary, either. Still as lonely and homesick as I was before the call, I determined to not read too much into the few words we had exchanged—knowing I would anyway— and headed into town.

Unbeknown to me, on the other side of the Irish Sea a few people were feeling unexpectedly encouraged. Being a habitually quiet and reticent person, Shonagh had opted to keep her feelings to herself for the time being and had mentioned me to no one. So by the time she returned to the table, her parents had developed an understandable amount of curiosity.

"Who was that?" her father asked.

"It was Michael," she said, concentrating on her meal. "He just wanted to say 'Hi.'"

"Michael?"

"A man I met on holiday."

Silence then, during which, I expect, her mother and father mentally high-fived each other and began planning what to do with Shonagh's room when she moved out.

But no one said a word. Instead, after a few minutes of silence, her father said, as if musing to himself.

"Well...I'd keep in touch."

Meanwhile, in Killarney, the late afternoon remained sunny and hot, bringing hordes of people onto the streets, which were narrow and choked with parked cars. Like Limerick, the buildings were squat, but painted, as they were, in bright colors and adorned with flower baskets, there was no somberness about the place. The people, too, were lively and friendly, apparently intent on enjoying the suddenly un-Irish-like weather. Downtown, the roads were wider and the sidewalks generous enough to allow street musicians and jugglers to entertain the crowds. The town was also laced with tiny lanes where cars could not go, and which led to shops and pubs or small courtyards with outdoor dining. I fell in love with the place immediately.

I explored for a while, soaking up the festive mood of the town, and eventually entered a pub at random. It claimed to be "traditional" and was named "O'Connor's" so I figured it was a good bet. The interior was roomy, comfortably cool after the heat of the street and populated by a handful of locals. Satisfied that I had made an astute choice, I took a table in the corner. As I was the only outsider there, I attracted a bit of attention. They were curious as to why I kept scribbling in my notebook and, at one point, a man wandered over to me, took a puff of my cigar, nodded his approval and went back to his seat, all without saying a word.

Their curiosity wasn't hostile; they displayed a friendly, almost playful attitude and, after they saw that I wasn't a threat to the serenity they had obviously been enjoying before my arrival, they pretty much left me alone. Then they started singing. They didn't sing as a group, or in any organized fashion, instead, one person would spontaneously start singing, and the rest of us would listen. They all sang well; the songs were of the folk variety—haunting and melancholic—and as the singer finished, there was no applause, just a quiet contemplation and maybe a few words of commentary. I felt I was on to something.

During one lull, I started singing, dredging up one of the many American/Irish folks songs I knew. This surprised them, not only the singing but the revelation that I was an American. After that, I was adopted by them, and the singing and drinking continued.

I stayed for the rest of the evening, chatting, singing and enjoying the ambiance as the pub filled up with locals. This, I realized, was what I had been looking for; there were no Budweiser bottles on display, no gaggles of tourists and no collection of eager youngsters playing crappy pseudo-Irish music for them. In fact, I don't recall any music at all, except for the singing that continued sporadically throughout the evening.

I met and befriended about a dozen people, then promptly allowed them to become lost in the alcoholic haze. At one point, while I was engaging in an animated conversation with my new best friend, the bartender shouted for last orders. The bar was full and we were all having a grand time—plus it wasn't all that late—and I felt it a shame that it would have to come to such an abrupt end. But then the bartender locked the front door, opened a side door and the revelry continued unabated. I was familiar with the term "lock in" but this was the first I had seen it employed in Ireland, and I was part of it.

We carried on for some time after and I walked back to the hotel in the late hours elated and satisfied. The Ireland I had hoped for, the Ireland that had, until now, lived only in my imagination and the nostalgia-laced memories of my Irish-American friends, had at last become real; I had found Ireland, I could call my trip a success, and I still had a full day to go.

The Ring of Kerry

The next day, the sun was up early. I, however, was not. By the time I roused myself and prepared for action, the day was already bright and hot and the sun had climbed high in the cloudless sky. Killarney was going to be very, very warm, but that hardly mattered as I had a plan that would take me into the countryside.

One of the many people I met the previous evening was an American. Not a tourist, but an actual immigrant. The conversation was fascinating and informative; here was a man who had done what I had been proposing to do (that would be move to Ireland, not escape from a control-freak girlfriend) and he didn't find the idea the least bit intimidating, complex or crazy. In fact, he assured me it was relatively easy. You would, of course, need to be totally committed to the idea and display a certain amount of tenacity, but overall, it was certainly doable. And a lot of people were doing it.

I found this revelation to be gratifying as well as vindicating; my notion, while a bit extreme, had not been so foolish after all. Had events turned out differently, I would have been able to escape to Ireland if I had so desired. By this juncture, of course, it was moot, so this revelation, while welcome, was not as intriguing or, ultimately, as useful as the other bit of advice he offered: I should not leave Ireland without touring the Ring of Kerry. Furthermore, I should not be tempted by the plentiful bus excursions on offer; it would, he advised, be a steeply superior experience if I took my own car.

He assured me that the route was so well-traveled and clearly delineated that getting lost would be impossible, a remark that prompted me to think that, even though he was my current best friend, he did not know me very well.

This was one of the few snatches of conversation that took place after the bartender locked the door that I could, with reasonable clarity, recall. The route for the Ring of Kerry went right through Killarney—I had seen signs for it—so I already knew where I was going. All I had to do was drive out of town one way and follow the route signs until I hit the town again.

Accordingly, after brunch, I got in my car and followed the Ring of Kerry signs northward out of town. Fortunately, the trail led to the left at the first roundabout so I managed to remain on the proper route for the first ten minutes. It went slightly downhill after that. What I hadn't told my new American friend the previous evening (not that I recall, anyway) and what I hadn't thought about myself, was the trip I had taken with my sons to Gettysburg, Pennsylvania.

In July of 1998, during that period of my life when I was not only looking for interesting things to do with three teenage boys, but scrambling for excuses to remain outside of She-Who-Must-Not-Be-Named's sphere of influence for as long as possible, I hit upon the idea of a trip to the Gettysburg battlefield. We spent a day driving down, booked into a scenic motel along the Interstate highway and, the next day, set out on a morning as bright and blue and warm as this one to discover the history scattered throughout the surrounding countryside. To assist us on our way, we had a battlefield tour map with the route clearly marked as well as a taped commentary that, when started at the correct point, would guide you through the route, telling you where and when to turn. Add to this the fact that the roads themselves were signposted—and signposted for tourists, no less, who are a special breed of stupid, as we proved time and again.

Naturally, we got lost. Repeatedly. No matter how many times we worked our way back to the route, we would lose it before the next farmstead came into view.

And so it was with the Ring of Kerry. I'd love to blame the unfamiliarity of the culture, or the driving on the wrong side of the road, or the tour buses that kept coming at me on the impossibly narrow roads and forcing me into the hedges, but despite the fact that all of those distractions were present, I know in my heart that, if they had not been, I would still have lost my way. It is simply what I do.

So in a rather zigzag manner, I managed to make it about a third of the way around the ring before I saw someone hitchhiking. The gods once again smiled upon me as the young man (who introduced himself as Matté; pronounced ma-TAY) not only knew the way around the ring and back to Killarney, but offered to guide me to the best lookout stops, as well—stops the tour buses were too big to get into. I gratefully accepted his offer and we began our leisurely, and less harried, drive around the Ring of Kerry.

Driving short distances, stopping and getting out to walk around kept my leg from acting up, and I was able to display my window lowering prowess to Matté, which, I am sure, impressed him. My expatriate friend's advice to take the car coupled with the fortuitous encounter with Matté made the trip a far superior experience than it would have been had I subjected myself to a bus tour; the views from the lesser-traveled overlook sites that Matté directed me to were stunning. When we pulled into the first lot, I was simply awestruck by the grandeur, the emerald beauty, the Irishness of it all. The next overlook showed me a scene even more grand and stunning, one that could never be equaled, until we moved on to the next beauty spot.

It was around this time that I began feeling sorry for the Irish; their country was so incredibly, consistently, monotonously beautiful that it surely must fade into the background. It had to; the alternative was to spend your life walking around going, "Holy shit! Look at that beautiful scenery!" I had to admit that I was already feeling as if seeing one more sweeping vista or chocolate-box village or quaint cottage was going to push me over the edge. And where, if you grow up surrounded by all this beauty, do you go on vacation? Living in Albany, I could go to Ireland and marvel at the splendor, but if I lived in Killarney where could I possibly go? Bayonne, New Jersey, just to get some contrast?

With Matté as my guide, we made it back to Killarney before midnight. In fact, it was still fairly early in the day, so to thank him, I treated him to lunch. As we ate, he told me he was from Slovenia and was backpacking around Europe. I pretended I knew where that was (Slovenia, not Europe) but I suspected it was one of the former Soviet Republics and, if so, that would make Matté the first bona fide communist (or former communist) I had ever spoken to. For all that, he seemed cordial enough; we had a nice meal and a good chat during which he never once tried to indoctrinate me. After lunch he thanked me for my hospitality and I him for his services, and we parted ways.

I returned to my hotel room to prepare for my early morning departure and to plot my course so I could get back to Shannon airport on time without getting hopelessly lost. Given my driving experiences of the past few days, I was not feeling very confident about the trip. My flight was at two o'clock so I needed to check in by noon, which meant getting the car back no later than eleven thirty, which meant I had to leave, well, I had no idea. The trip was only about 90 miles, a distance I could comfortably cover in an hour and a half in the US, but in Ireland, that might take me half the day. I decided to leave as early as I could, just to be safe.

The only activity I had to decide on after that was what to do with my last night in Ireland. It occurred to me that, although I had hit the milestones I had hoped for in this trip, I did not yet have a photo of me enjoying a pint of Guinness in an authentic, Irish pub to take back as a souvenir. So, after dinner, I returned to O'Connor's Pub. I harbored no illusions of a repeat of the previous night's gaiety, but seeing as how it was the place where I had enjoyed my most satisfying "Irish moments," I thought it an appropriate place to see if I could talk a waiter or kind patron into taking my photo.

It was still relatively early, so the pub was deserted when I arrived. I ordered a Guinness from the red-haired barmaid, lit up a cigar and quietly waited for the evening crowd to show up. The barmaid wasn't the quiet type, however; she was spunky, with a wicked sense of humor and set about giving me a hard time about my cigar. After we bantered back and forth a few minutes, she told me she was in such a happy mood because some customers who had left just before I arrived had been visitors who lived in her hometown, so she had gotten all the local family news and gossip. I asked her where home was. She named a town that meant nothing to me.

"It's in Scotland," she said. "I've been in Killarney so long I've lost me accent."

Then she told me her name was Shonagh.

"Not Shauna, like the locals here think. It's Shonagh, S-H-"

"O-N-A-G-H," I finished for her. She was openly surprised that I knew how to spell it.

"Before last week," I told her, "I'd never heard that name before. Now you're the second Shonagh I've met on this trip."

134

"And the first?"

"An English woman I met."

Her eyes sparkled mischievously. "Had a little holiday romance, did we now?"

"No," I said, "I think it's more than that. But now she's back in England and I'm stuck here."

"Oh, so it's love sick you are, now? I'll put on some love songs for ya."

Thankfully, the pub began to fill up after that. It started as a trickle, with a few locals—but none I recognized—drifting in for an evening pint, then it turned into a torrent of tourists: clusters of Americans, which made me homesick, bevies of Brits, which made me miss Shonagh, scatterings of Germans and even some Japanese. The evening bar staff arrived and my new friend, Shonagh the barmaid, left. Then some musicians arrive—a grizzled old woman with a banjo and a guitar and an equally grizzled old man with an accordion. I groaned inwardly; the duo was reminiscent of the ensemble I had had the misfortune of enduring in the pub in Ouhterard, and my hopes for a pleasant evening fell like a careless tourist hiking the slippery slopes of Croagh Patrick.

I had thought the pub was crowded the night before, but on this night, there was barely any standing room. I was glad I had arrived early so I could get a seat, but now I was being jammed up against the bar. The noise level rose as more and more drinks passed over the bar and into the crowd. The pub was becoming so raucous and packed that, if I did manage to talk someone into taking my photo, there wouldn't be enough room to back away from the camera. All I was likely to get would be a photo of the Guinness logo on my shirt. I considered leaving to find a quieter place, then the band started to play.

I had never associated the accordion with Irish music, but the old guy made it work, and his partner on the guitar complimented his tune with a driving background rhythm. They sang traditional Irish ballads, not diddly-dee Disney nonsense, in melodious voices edged with Celtic roughness. I ordered another Guinness and started singing and shouting along with the crowd.

For a couple of old folks, they had amazing energy, and played song after song for over an hour before taking a break. I seized the advantage of relative quiet and began chatting with the couple sitting next to me. They were from Philadelphia, and hearing this made me inexplicably homesick. We traded stories about our Irish experiences but before I could ask them to take my photo, the band started up again.

The crowd had thinned out during the break, leaving the pub simply full as opposed to packed, which made listening to the music even more enjoyable. The remaining crowd—the die-hards—were of course the more enthusiastic of the fans, so the noise level did not drop in proportion to the depletion of the audience. There was singing and whooping and shouted encouragements as the duo performed ballad after ballad. I became so caught up in the excitement that, when they started singing a melody I recalled from dance class, I went up to the empty spot in front of the band and started dancing an Irish jig. Admittedly, two weeks without practice and the unknown quantity of Guinness I had consumed took the polish off my steps, but the crowd didn't seem to mind. They hooted and cheered—although, to be fair, I probably could have gone up there and done the Hokey-Pokey and gotten as much applause—while I was simply happy to have finished the dance without once falling over.

Before I could return to my seat, one of the bartenders who had been on duty the previous day recognized me as the singing American, and asked if I would do a song.

So I did. I sang *The Parting Glass*, as it seemed an appropriate song for both the evening and my trip. The audience cheered again when I finished (and not, I hope, *because* I'd finished) and I made it back to my seat this time, amid high-fives and handshakes.

By then the band, the crowd and the evening were winding down and, satisfied that my trip to Ireland was complete, I asked the Philadelphia couple to take my photo.

I left the pub shortly after for a quiet walk through the silent streets back to my hotel. Tomorrow I would be going home, back to my life, the questions that needed answering and the decisions that needed making, but that would have to wait—tonight was all about Ireland. I thought about the good times I'd had over the past dozen days, the amazing sights I'd seen, the wonderful people I'd met, the hideous weather I'd experienced and, of course, Shonagh. And I thought again of the premonition; had I found Ireland, had the Celtic spirit spoken to me, was I going to leave my heart here? Or had it, instead, traveled to England?

Leaving Ireland

My final morning in Ireland, like the few before it, dawned clear and warm and portentous of a hot day. I woke early, feeling no sense of melancholy, nostalgia, regret or, indeed, any other emotion beyond an urgency to get to the airport on time. I packed, double-checked to make sure I had left nothing behind, double-checked again, had a quick breakfast and hit the road.

The trip looked promising: on my way out of Killarney, I found, and successfully followed, signs pointing the way to Limerick. Limerick was only 25 miles from the airport and, if it came to the worst, I could always abandon the car there and take the bus. I had, I realized, finally reached a place where I wasn't totally out of my depth and felt confident that I could find the airport with little difficulty. Still, when you're handed an advantage, you don't pass it up, so when I saw an elderly gentleman in a tweed jacket and a flat cap hitchhiking outside of Farranfore, I picked him up.

His name was Liam, he was on his way to Limerick and he talked non-stop the entire way. I didn't mind; he not only provided excellent directions but also offered a running commentary on every town, village and hamlet we passed through as well as some interesting insights into life in Ireland as seen through the eyes of someone who has been around awhile. He was very taken with the new Ireland and the wonders that prosperity had brought with it, especially the upgraded road system.

"Five year ago, ye would'na have this good a road here," he told me. "It would be very narrow and the going slower."

And sometime later, as we approached a bridge, he pointed it out with rising excitement. "See that!" he said. "That there carry over, it's actually got a *road* on it. There's a road up there, maybe going to Kerry or someplace. It's a Godsend, I tell ya!"

We passed beneath it, Liam beaming, me thinking, "It's just a bridge, for chrissake!"

As we passed through Adare, I learned that President Clinton had stayed there once, and in nearly every town he pointed out the local church:

"That there is the (insert suitably religious name here) Church," he would say, crossing himself as we passed by.

At one point, he began effusing about detached housing. This was a concept I had picked up on during my first few days in Ireland, but it was still alien to me. In America, a house is a house. If your house happened to be attached to another house, you called it a duplex, and if it was one of a row of houses, you referred to it as a town house (you did; your friends and relatives called it an apartment behind your back). But if you said "house," it was understood to mean a single, stand-alone home. In Ireland, an unencumbered house was not a given, so if you were fortunate enough to live in one, you let people know by referring to it as a "detached" house.

Still, I didn't think they were rare enough to merit such interest. Liam talked about them for miles.

"That village I told you about, the one with detached houses, it's coming up after this next town."

He interjected these remarks this into his monologue like a kid counting down the miles to a Six

Flags amusement park. When, at last, the detached houses came into view, he pointed them out as we passed by.

"Look!" he said. "There they are! Detached houses!"

I glanced to my left and saw, not a modern development of American-style homes, but a tidy row of ancient Irish cottages, all with thatched roofs. Apparently he had been saying, "the thatched houses," and I understood at once that it was time for me to go home.

Liam got out near Limerick, but he put me on the Shannon road where all I had to do was follow signs for the airport. It was with some regret that I watched him walk away; he was fascinating company, and the last real Irish person I was likely to talk to. I spent the rest of my journey in silence.

I knew I was getting close to the airport when my leg began throbbing. The increase in traffic meant more time on the clutch and after the Ring of Kerry and my tour of south western Ireland, my knee had about had enough. And so had I. Up ahead I saw a gas station, but I still had a ways to go; certainly there would be others before I arrived at the car rental. So I passed it by, and brought the car back empty. It cost me fifty pounds but by then I was beyond caring.

I did care about getting dinged for the minor damage caused by the shrubs that had attacked the car. After a close inspection, and the application of some spit and elbow grease, I convinced the young woman that it was all superficial markings that would wash off. And I'm sure it was, really; I'm just glad she didn't look at the passenger's side wing mirror too closely.

After that, I went through the process of Americanization. First I changed my Irish pounds back into dollars, and then—as I passed through customs and security, alternately assuring them I had nothing of value to declare and had certainly not been walking around near farmland so if I could avoid the cavity search and/or being hosed down with disinfectant, I would appreciate it very much, thank you—the mixture of accents went from full-on Irish, to a smattering of Asian and European and, finally, upon making myself comfortable at the bar nearest to my departure gate, predominantly American.

My fellow passengers and I did the boarding dance (more of a shuffle, actually) onto the Aer Lingus flight going direct to Boston; no Heathrow detour on this end of the trip, just a straight shot home. We taxied a short distance, then the engines roared and the pressure clamped me to my seat as the plane accelerated for takeoff. Ironically, this was becoming one of my favorite parts of flying—if it can be said that flying holds a favorite part at all—despite it being one of the two most dangerous moments of air travel. (The other is landing, my hands down favorite part.) But dangerous or not, I found myself enjoying the thrill of acceleration and the surreal feeling of lifting into the air and watching the ground fall further and further behind. Then, of course, panic took over.

Unlike our landing, we left Ireland through a crystal sky and as we gained altitude I could see below me the Cliffs of Moher, the Aran Islands and the fetching landscape I had come to know so intimately. Despite my longing to be home, I felt an ache of regret, but just a small one; although my Ireland adventure was now behind me, many more awaited. I then attempted to project myself six hours through time, to that moment when my favorite part of flying was over and I would be safely back on firm ground.

It was Tuesday, the 28th of August, 2001. Resigning myself to the journey, I settled into my seat and let the plane carry me back to America, my uncertain future and a world that was about to change.

Part III
Denouement

The plane touched down at Logan at eight o'clock that evening, although the clocks in the airport assured me it was only three in the afternoon. From there I caught a commuter flight to Albany where I was picked up by my friend, Jeanne, the same person who had dropped me off two weeks earlier; fitting bookends to my fantasy.

During the short ride to my apartment, I filled her in on all the adventures I'd had and the sights I'd seen; most of them, at least. I kept quiet about Shonagh, fearing to mention her lest giving voice to the experience might somehow pervert it. As it was now, clear and fresh in my mind, it remained pure and full of potential. But once I let it out for others to assess and paw over, it might diminish, or show itself to have been nothing more than a vacation fling after all. Perhaps this was why Shonagh had kept quiet, preferring to hold onto the memories rather than share them.

So I told her about The Death March, and the bogs, and the stunning Cliffs of Moher, and if I seemed excessively ebullient, that was probably due to the excitement of the trip.

Back in my apartment, I began the process of unpacking and winding down from a long and exciting vacation. It was early evening, or nearly midnight, depending on which clock you favored, but despite the hour, when a friend called and asked me to meet him for a drink, he didn't have to ask twice.

I met him around nine o'clock at a pub in Saratoga. He and his wife were sitting at a table in the outdoor seating area, enjoying one of the last serene evenings of summer. He asked about the trip and I began recalling some of my adventures when his wife interrupted:

"What's up with the ring?" she asked.

Busted; leave it to a woman to spot something like that.

"Remember that guy I told you about," I said, "the one I was going to hire to follow me around and kick me in the ass anytime I looked twice at a woman? Well, I couldn't afford a ticket for him so I left him behind when I went to Ireland."

And so I told them about Shonagh, and I discovered why I hadn't told Jeanne, and why I had conspired to keep it all inside: telling them did not diminish the experience, it made it real. Suddenly, Shonagh was no longer a fanciful feeling flitting around inside of me, but a tangible part of my life—one that demanded a decision.

For now, however, the retelling of my impossibly romantic story kept the demons at bay and there followed excited presumptions of transatlantic trips and, if things went well, of moving Shonagh to America to live with me. I nodded and smiled, knowing that would never be.

I—like my two friends and the others I told in the days that followed—grew up assuming that everyone in the rest of the world wanted, above all else, to come to America. The trip, if nothing more, had taught me otherwise. I was now aware that there were vast numbers of people beyond our borders who had no desire to live in the greatest nation on the planet; I didn't yet understand it, but I was at least aware of it, even if my friends were not. And furthermore, knowing

Shonagh as I did, I knew America was not for her; the fast pace, the vast distances and the isolation from her family would conspire to make her miserable. There would be no America for Shonagh, and I simply couldn't pack in a 25-year career in civil service, give up my apartment, sell my car and pop over to England. So therein lay the problem.

As I went to sleep that evening, fresh from the pub, with Shonagh's pound coin on my dresser and her ring on my finger, the giddy feeling remained. In the dark hours, however, I came suddenly awake with my blood cold in my veins and the question I had done my best to suppress screaming at me from the back of my mind.

What had I done to my life?

After fighting so hard to gain and maintain my independence, I had tossed it aside on a whim. I now not only had a girlfriend, but one who was three thousand miles away. (Although, given my track record, this probably wasn't the worst thing that could happen to me.) Having a girlfriend, however, obligated me; I didn't mind living alone so much as long as my life was my own. But now I had to behave as if I was in a relationship without any of the benefits. And when were we going to see each other? Transatlantic airline tickets do not grow on trees, so if we could only be together for a week or so once a year, what would be the point?

These and other questions kept me awake that night, and many nights after. The e-mails and phone calls Shonagh and I exchanged in the days that followed did nothing to help; there was a feeling there, a strong one, one we both wanted to explore, but neither of us had the answer to the question concerning the large body of water separating us, and neither of us wanted to end it.

We remained at an impasse, and the enormity of what was happening continued to haunt me. Then, one night some weeks later, I allowed the epiphany I had experienced—the one I was destined to discover, the one

I had stuffed into my mental sock drawer and tried to avoid—to seep into the forefront of my consciousness where I could assess it and, perhaps, make peace with it.

It had happened on the road to Lisdoonvarna, on that hot and heady day after the Cliffs of Moher and our lunch in Doolin. We were talking, continuing the non-stop data dump of our lives that we had been engaging in for the past few days, when the conversation came round to cricket. I knew little about cricket, but it turned out Shonagh didn't know very much more. She did, however, understand that they threw the ball differently than an American baseball player.

"The bowler gets way back," she said, going into a slight stoop and miming holding a cricket ball. "Then he runs forward and winds up." At this point she took a few steps and windmilled her arm, preparing to release the ball. "And he flings it at the wicket."

It happened the moment she released the pretend ball at the imaginary batter and invisible wicket: a certainty exploded inside me. In that instant, I knew, in a way that required no explanation and would suffer no denial, in a way that was physically infused into my make-up, in the way that I knew I was right-handed and had brown (or at least it used to be brown) hair: I was in love with her, deeply and irrevocably.

The thought stunned me, and I immediately sought to bury it, but I could not deny the truth it unveiled: I considered myself a good person, or at least a person who wanted to be good, but sometimes that wasn't easy for me, sometimes I found myself at odds with the person I was striving to become. And in that moment on that road I realized, while I was with Shonagh, I was the person I always wanted to be, and I knew then that we were destined for each other. Though our paths had intersected only for those few, brief days in that remote land, our lives had become inexorably intertwined; a connection had been made, and it would not be broken.

I examined that buried feeling now and let the knowledge ease my mind; we had set a wheel in motion on that lazy Irish afternoon, and it would turn and scoop us up and carry us with it. Where, I had no way of knowing, all I knew was that Shonagh and I, wherever we were, wherever we ended up, would be together.

I slept that night with an easy mind, as I have every night since.

Epilogue

Reader, I married her.

About the Author

Michael Harling grew up in rural Columbia County in Upstate New York. He moved to the UK in March 2002 and has been recording his observations of the indigenous population on his popular blog *Postcards From Across the Pond* ever since.

Michael is the father of three sons from a previous marriage. He currently lives in Sussex.

For Michael's blog, website and contact details, visit:
www.michaelharling.com

Follow Michael's further adventures in:

POSTCARDS *from across* THE POND

and

MORE POSTCARDS *from across* THE POND

Excerpts from *Postcards* and
More Postcards*

Getting There

My great-grandfather, according to family legend, was deported from England. For all I know, this may be true; a story as splendid as this discourages scrutiny and can only diminish if mixed with mundane distractions such as facts. It's also largely irrelevant. Whether my ancestors jumped or were pushed, they left Blighty without a backward glance. No one, to my knowledge, had returned to the mother country and I, a second-generation Republican, wasn't about to break tradition, especially with a solid career, a spacious apartment in the suburbs and a comfortable future to look forward to in America. Emigration is for third worlders looking for a better life; Americans know there is no better life anywhere else and stay put.

I wasn't searching for anything more than a bit of sightseeing when I took my first trip abroad in August 2001. Yet six months later, I had quit my job, given up my apartment and was sitting on a transcontinental jet banking over the Sussex countryside for the final approach into Gatwick airport. The word "immigrant" never entered my mind—it has such a working class ring to it—but that's what I had become.

As the plane maneuvered toward the runway, the young woman in the seat next to me began siphoning off her rising excitement through conversation. She was an

American student on her first trip abroad, planning to stay for an unspecified time and hoping to pick up a job as an au pair. I nodded, making sympathetic noises and kept silent concerning the legal logistics her plan would require. At the time, I knew the immigration code by rote, but appearing too knowledgeable on the subject might draw suspicion and I couldn't afford to tip my hand; she might be a spy for the Home Office.

In truth, I was on my way to marry the British woman I had met on the aforementioned trip and had visited only twice since. This would be my final crossing; after the plane touched down (preferably right-side up and on the runway) I had no intention of leaving the United Kingdom. Assuming, of course, they let me in.

The idea that being an American didn't automatically allow me to go wherever I pleased whenever it pleased me was still a novel and shocking concept. I had, after all, visited Mexico, Canada and several Caribbean Islands without benefit of a passport, so it came as something of a surprise when—on my introductory visit—the Irish immigration clerk refused to admit me.

Subsequent visits found me better prepared, but my current trip was a bit more, how should I phrase this, delicate. At that time, coming into Britain to marry someone wasn't exactly illegal, but it was highly suspect. The odds of me being fingered for contriving a marriage of convenience just so I could enjoy the copious benefits of being a UK resident were admittedly low, but there remained the real chance I might be turned away by a cranky Immigration clerk who was still upset that they allowed Madonna in. And once turned away, getting back in could prove difficult indeed. Therefore, I had decided on the safer route: obfuscation.

My carry-on, as well as my suitcase, contained no photo albums, mementos or anything else that might suggest an intention of staying longer than two weeks. I had an appropriately dated return ticket and a camera around my neck. I didn't have to worry about pretending to act like a bumbling tourist—that part came naturally.

With the plane safely docked and unloading, I wished my hopeful companion good fortune and followed the herd through the terminal to immigration. (I've always wondered how the first guy knows where to go; if I de-planed first, I'd probably lead everyone into the parking garage.)

Having been through Immigration Control at Gatwick before, I knew enough to eschew the fast lanes reserved for European Union members and instead joined the shorter, but slower, procession under the "All Other Countries" sign. The crossing was, from a journalistic point of view, disappointingly smooth; I told the immigration clerk where I would be staying, showed my return ticket and entered my new home.

The journey, since that time, has been perplexing, frustrating, surprising and, above all, continually infused with humor, which was why I began chronicling my adventures in this strange but pleasant land. Even now, I am still making surprising discoveries (just this morning I found out British children refer to "Chicken Little" of falling sky fame as "Chicken Licken," which, to my American ears, sounds vaguely pornographic) and continue to be grateful that I have not yet had to seek employment as an au pair.

Fun With Firearms

I grew up in rural America, and that means one thing (well, okay, two): cow tipping, and guns.

Firearms are as American as a Post Office massacre and, where I grew up, chambering a round was as natural a part of life as sneaking bottles of beer out of the back of my sister's boyfriend's pickup truck while she gave him a hand-job in the cab. I learned to shoot when I was nine and rarely encountered anyone who didn't own a gun. It was, therefore, expected that I would acquire my own guns as I grew up, providing my sister's boyfriend didn't shoot me first.

Because of this upbringing, as well as several peripheral yet not unimportant activities, I found myself, some years later, living in suburban America with a wife, three infant children, a loaded pistol in the night table and a burglar creeping up the stairs.

Well, that's what it sounded like, anyway. My erstwhile wife and I were reading in bed late one night when we both detected the sound of furtive footsteps on the stairway. We barely had time to exchange startled looks before the noise sounded again and convinced us there was someone in the house.

While I freely admit to being a devout coward, sometimes a man's gotta do what a man's gotta do, and so, with a mildly trembling heart, I slipped out of bed, grabbed the pistol, scooped up the sleeping cat and went to confront the intruder.

Looking back, I suppose the sight of a naked man holding a revolver in one hand and a bewildered feline in the other might have been enough to convince any would-be burglar to vacate the premises voluntarily, especially if the man said something enigmatic and

Eastwood-esque, such as "I've got a cat here, mister, and I'm not afraid to use it."

Instead, desiring to keep the element of surprise firmly in my corner, I tiptoed to the edge of the doorway and flung the startled cat into the abyss, the theory being that a yowling, hissing sprawl of fur, claws and teeth would initiate an interesting diversion and provide cover for my next move, which was to jump into the hallway, assume the official police firing position (learned from watching episodes of TJ Hooker) and get the drop on an empty stairwell. Empty, that is, save for a confused cat lying on the bottom riser, shaking her head and glaring up at me with a look that all but screamed, "And just what the hell was THAT all about?"

Despite the continued dearth of burglars, when I started the night shift, my wife insisted on transferring the pistol to her nightstand. Possessing a passing awareness of firearm safety, I was disturbingly conscious of the fact that the most likely person to become an unwilling target was myself, then my wife, children, neighbors, milkman, paper boy, visiting evangelists and way, way down the list, you might find a burglar. So when my wife left for work in the morning, I removed the bullets and loaded the revolver with blanks.

This kept the world a safer place, until she overheard me telling a friend about it at a party. As soon as we arrived home she frog marched me into the bedroom where—arms crossed, foot tapping—she scowled at me until I re-loaded the weapon. Seven hours later I reversed the process, restoring sanity, if not honesty, to a home rapidly filling up with curious toddlers.

To my wife's credit, she eventually relented and, recalling my own childhood pranks—such as removing the hinges from my father's locked gun cabinet to get at the hardware inside—I dismantled the guns and kept several key pieces secured in my desk at work, which was how things remained for many eventful, but thankfully firearm-free, years.

It wasn't until my move to the UK that I discovered pistols are like children; you continue to be responsible for them until you can convince someone else to take them off your hands. I was surprised at the paperwork involved in getting rid of these idle hunks of metal but, after accomplishing this task, I felt strangely unburdened, as if a 20-something son suddenly abandoned his dreams of becoming a mime, got a proper job and moved out of the basement.

Although the UK, like everywhere else, has its bad element, I feel undeniably less likely to be shot here than back in my old hometown where every other citizen is packing heat. Cultural differences continue to surface and I find it amazing to the point of disbelief that my friends here have never handled, and in many cases have never even seen, a gun. Likewise, when they hear tales of how enamored we Americans are of our weapons, they, too, are incredulous, and just a little bit afraid.

They should be.

As for myself, I'm enjoying living in a gun-free (well, gun-reduced, anyway) society. Crimes may happen—that's simply a sad fact of life—but, at least if I do hear something go "bump" in the night, I won't be scrambling around in the dark with a loaded six-shooter.

In the interest of home security, however, I'm thinking about getting a cat.

Push / Pull

I recently read that Britain has the highest failure rate for Americans attempting to relocate anyplace other than America. I'm not surprised. After all, if you decide to settle in Timbuktu, you expect life to be exotic and difficult; but Britain, that's really like the US, right?

Wrong. On the surface, it appears to be a quaint copy of its former colony, but you soon find everything about the place—not most things, everything—is just off-center enough to give you a sense of permanent imbalance, where even the most mundane of tasks becomes an opportunity for bewilderment or embarrassment or both.

Mailing a letter, for instance.

Back in the US, when I mailed letters to the UK, I walked into a Post Office, handed my letters to the clerk and said, "These need postage to the UK." It seemed reasonable, therefore, to assume a similar scenario should play out in Britain. So, with letters in hand, I set out to locate a Post Office.

I was informed there was one in a nearby parade, which, after some confusion, I discovered means a strip mall in Britain. Finding the parade was easy enough, but after wandering past a chippie, an Indian take-away, a DIY Center, a Kebab shop and an Off License, I still found no place to leave my letters.

A more rigorous search turned up the Post Office, housed inside another store. In the far corner of the News Agent (a sort of magazine stand cum convenience market) I spotted something that looked like a ticket booth under a sign reading "Royal Mail", so I walked up to the woman inside the booth and slid my letters through the slot.

"These need postage to the US," I said.

She regarded me with a look that fell slightly short of annoyance and slid them back.

"You have to weigh them first," she told me, pointing at a scale sitting on the ledge outside her window. I obliged her.

"One at a time," she sighed.

Again, I obliged her.

"Sixty-eight pence, forty-five pence, sixty-eight pence. And you'll need some air mail stickers."

I slid my money, along with the letters, once again, through the slot.

She slid them back, with the stamps and blue airmail stickers on top.

"Next!" she said to the empty store.

I retreated to the sweets and crisps aisle with my DIY mail where I somewhat awkwardly assembled it, then returned to the street in search of a mailbox. The search went on for some time but became much easier once I was made to understand that mailboxes in Britain aren't big, blue and square but, instead, resemble overgrown fire hydrants.

Another source of confusion springs from the rather reluctant way Brits put numbers on their businesses. Thirty-Two Broadway is a seemingly foolproof address, but upon arrival at Broadway I discovered an alarming lack of numbered buildings and was left with no alternative except to start where One should be and count up to 32. (Thankfully, I have not yet had occasion to apply for a job with a company housed at 2165 Park Lane.)

Counting up to my destination seemed a brilliant solution until it occurred to me having a company receptionist watching a bewildered American counting doorways and then stopping in front of her building doesn't exactly improve that American's employment potential, especially when the American in question can't figure out how to open the door.

You see, doors open differently here. They do not uniformly swing outward, as they do in the States. Mostly they open inward, but not always. As a result, I'm forever trying to pull doors open when I should be pushing, and vice-versa. Signs offering helpful suggestions such as "PUSH" or "PULL" might reduce these incidents, but they are so rare it isn't worth stopping to look for one. Therefore, I repeatedly yanked on the door handle in a fruitless effort to pull it open until it belatedly occurred to me to push. As I entered the lobby I wondered that the receptionist hadn't already called her boss: "Your one o'clock is here, Mr. Jones. This shouldn't take long, he's a bit of a plonker."

The interview went about as well as you might expect, and lasted just long enough for me to forget that the door opened inward, affording me the opportunity of flashing my winning, "I'm not really an idiot, please hire me" smile at the receptionist before slamming face first into the unyielding door. Flustered, I reached for the handle—it was right there next to the big, red sign reading, "PULL"—and opened the door.

As I left, I swear I heard the receptionist mumble into her intercom something about my application form and the document shredder.

Married & Driving

This past week, I got married, which means, among other incidental legalities, that I can now lawfully drive my wife's car.

To me, driving is a deeply ingrained instinct. Owning a car isn't a privilege; it's a birthright, as much a part of what being an American is all about as firearms and fast-food franchises. Finding myself, for the first time in recent memory, without a vehicle or the legal right to drive one left me with a vague yet pervasive sense of incompleteness, like the feeling you get when you arrive at the office and realize you've forgotten to put on underwear. It also forced me to acquire skills unparalleled in most American's experiences, such as learning to read a bus timetable and appreciating the joys of walking.

Surprisingly, I find I enjoy being a pedestrian in England. Europe is infinitely more cordial to non-automobile traffic than America, primarily, because the proximity of everything makes walking a viable option. But just as important, public transportation, beyond the confines of the continental United States, isn't regarded as the sole reserve of recently released felons and people too poor or brain damaged to own a car. The ability to actually get somewhere and not have to worry about where you're going to put your car once you arrive is, I have discovered, an enjoyable and liberating experience.

On the other hand, I am an American, and that means I will—if I possibly can—drive. Which was why, immediately following our wedding, I convinced my wife we were in dire need of a liter of milk and found myself seated in what I consider to be the passenger's side of the car, facing traffic on a busy street traveling on the wrong side of the road.

The theory behind driving on the left isn't hard to grasp, but the actual execution leaves you feeling as if you arrived at the office and remembered your underwear, but it's on backward; the familiar is suddenly foreign and the simplest maneuvers can cause confusion or embarrassment and possess the potential of personal injury. It takes some time to become comfortable with the notion that all those cars coming at you are not, at the last moment, going to swerve into your lane and try to pass you on the left. But that's not nearly as frightening as realizing you are subconsciously planning the exact maneuver and are much more likely to attempt it in a moment of inappropriate patriotism.

The second most obvious difference is the positioning of the car itself, not on the road, but around you. In America, there is much more car on your right, but in the UK, the bulk of the automobile extends to your left, often up onto the pavement or into roadside bushes. This can be distressing to passengers, as I discovered from the occasional yelp emanating from my wife's direction.

Another interesting feature of UK driving is the roundabout. We call them rotaries in the US (or "traffic circles" if you live in Latham, New York) and they are found mostly in the New England states. After building a few there, they realized they didn't work and put traffic lights up in the rest of the country. Europe, slow to catch on, or addicted to the adrenaline rush, continues to use roundabouts.

I'm told that roundabouts aren't inherently dangerous and can genuinely aid traffic flow, if everybody using them understands and follows the rules. Needless to say, I am a little light in the understanding department. Acquainted with the four-way stop, I simply assumed the first person at the roundabout had the right of way. I'm happy to report the brakes tested very well on our car, as did the horns on several others.

Then my wife told me to take a right. So I did. How was I to know that meant turning to the left and driving three quarters of the way around the circle to exit on the road to my right? It seemed much quicker and simpler to turn right but my wife insisted so I turned left and exited onto the wrong road.

Fortunately, you never have to drive very far in our town before you come to another roundabout, and one thing they excel at is facilitating U-turns.

Shortly after that, I was introduced to ZEB-ra crossings.

ZEB-ra is British for Zebra, because they pronounce "Z" as "ZED," something that, prior to this, had escaped my notice. (And, once it was brought to my attention, all I could think was, "Then how do they sing the 'Zorro' song?" Somehow, "Zorro, the fox so cunning and freeeee, Zorro, who makes the sign of the ZED" just doesn't pan.)

A Zebra Crossing, therefore, is a series of white stripes painted across the street; you can see the Beatles walking across one on the cover of the Abbey Road album. Apparently, the rule is, if you are a pedestrian and you step onto the street within the confines of these white stripes, automobile drivers are not supposed to run you over. Traffic stopping for pedestrians is an exotic concept to me so, in the absence of a red light or cranky policeman blowing a whistle and holding up his hand, I carried on.

When my wife shouted, "ZEB-ra crossing!" the words meant absolutely nothing to me, but the tone suggested I stop. So I did.

Several pedestrians ambled by, after which my wife—accompanied by the cars behind me who hadn't had the chance to test their horns in the roundabout— encouraged me to move along.

It was then, as I meandered the wrong way up the one-way lanes of the shopping center's car park, that I received my education regarding ZED's and ZEE's and pedestrian right-of-way.

When we eventually made it inside the store, I changed my mind about the milk and bought a half-case of Guinness instead.

And my wife drove home. At my request.

On Becoming Legal

It's dark when we leave the house, but already it promises to be a warm, clear day. On the train ride north, the sky tinges pink and dawn creeps over the horizon as we walk through the sleepy streets of Croydon toward the Home Office. It isn't hard to find, we just look for the queue.

At 6:50 AM, we are the fortieth in line. We weave our way through the cattle barriers under the covered queuing area and wait. By 7:30 the cattle barriers are packed and the queue snakes down the sidewalk. About that time, a beefy security guard appears and, in a broad, south London accent, orders us to tighten up the line. His accent is so thick and unfamiliar that I can't understand a word he says. If not for my wife, I couldn't know what he wants us to do. I can't imagine the others are having much more luck understanding him, but the group, as a whole, manages to grasp his meaning and we all scrunch up together, allowing the maximum number of people into the cattle barriers.

"Pklyd yrthg ejdhmk s jdkhme gfy," he says as he walks away.

I turn to my wife. "What did he say?"

"He said, 'Make friends, it's going to be a long day.'"

At eight o'clock we still have an hour to wait and my wife feels a sudden desire for the loo. We have plenty of time, so she slips out of line and goes in search of some facilities.

Almost immediately we begin to move. The security guards at the front of the barriers count off groups of petitioners and herd them through the massive revolving doors of the Home Office. I shuffle forward. Another group is counted and herded. I shuffle forward.

163

Another group. No sign of my wife. The next group. No wife. Now it's my turn. Do I try to explain to them? They don't look like they are in the mood for a chat, so I allow them to herd me through the rotating door. I'm inside, my wife is outside.

I am processed, x-rayed and searched in much the same manner as I might be at Kennedy Airport if I showed up with a sawed-off twelve gauge in my carry on. After I'm cleared for entry, I find myself in another queue, and then I'm facing a large African man behind a thick panel of glass.

"Kjdufy jkfdu ndhegf," he says.

"Uh, I'm here to get a visa?" I try.

"Kjdufy jkfdu ndhegf!"

"Um, I just got married. I'm here for a marriage visa?"

"Kjdufy jkfdu ndhegf!!"

"The one year visa?"

"KJDUFY JKFDU NDHEGF!!!"

It's no use. He rips off a number, scrawls something on the back and hands it to me. I walk away with the prize. We are number 40 in the queue but, at the moment, we aren't even in the building. I hustle up the stairs to the second floor as instructed and ask the security unit there what I am supposed to do next.

"Go to the second floor," they tell me.

"But, this is the second floor!"

"This is the first floor. Down there is the ground floor. Up those stairs, that's the second floor."

I've been on my own for all of ten minutes and already I'm floundering. I've got to get my wife back.

Up what is properly the third floor but which the Brits refer to as the second floor, I show my number to the security unit and explain that I have lost my wife.

"Can I go out and look for her?" I ask.

"Yes," they tell me, "but when you come back in you have to get in the back of the queue."

"But I already went through the line. I have my number."

"If you leave the building, you have to go to the back of the queue."

It's no use. I do the only thing I can, which is stand as close as possible to the rotating door while more cattle are herded in. I wait and watch and hope.

Soon I see her, frantically pleading with (thank God) a female security guard. She allows my wife to move up in the queue. She sees me waving. She slips through the revolving door with the rest of the cattle.

After processing, we're back together. Much relieved, we head for the stairs. The ground floor security unit inspects my ticket.

"This is for one person only," they tell us. "Only one of you can go up."

"But we were separated when I got the ticket. We were in line together."

"Only one of you can go up."

We rejoin the indoor queue and find a window without a large, African man sitting behind it. Instead, there is a petit, African woman there, and she cheerfully changes the numeral one on my ticket to a two.

The room on the second floor is massive and resembles the deck of an extremely crowded and low-budget cruise ship. The blue bench seats, in neat, nautical rows, are bolted to the concrete floor; at the far end of the room is an open, empty area where I wouldn't be surprised to find a shuffleboard court. Twenty-five clerk windows, all fitted with riot-proof glass, face the benches. Security guards are everywhere.

It looks like a meeting of the United Nations (or at least a meeting of the maintenance staff of the United Nations) with all manner of nationalities represented. We are ordered to sit. The room, though filling to the brim, is reverently hushed. They begin calling numbers at 8:30.

We don't have long to wait. It's not yet ten o'clock when our number is called. We approach confidently, our paperwork in a neat binder with plenty of supporting documentation.

The woman behind the counter, a large, Afro-Caribbean woman, looks at all our papers. She is particularly interested in my passport with its numerous stamps and markings. She studies our application.

"It says here you decided to get married last October."

"Yes, that's right."

"But you returned to the States after that," she says, eyeing me suspiciously. "Why didn't you get a Fiancée Visa?"

"Um...I...I was advised I didn't need one."

"You're supposed to have a Fiancée Visa."

"I, er, didn't think I needed one."

"You were back in the US; you were supposed to get one before you returned to the UK."

"I just...we didn't...the tourist visa, I came in on a Tourist Visa and we just...got married."

Her eyes accuse me.

"I thought that would be all right," I finish lamely.

She abruptly loses interest.

"Take a seat. I'll call you when I'm ready for you."

Our minds whirl with fantasies of security guards bursting in to the room, brandishing weapons, to handcuff me and ship me back to the States on a container vessel. The woman disappears with our documents into another room. We take our seats and wait, the fantasies growing more vivid and grotesque with each long minute. As my mind begins to involuntarily entertain thoughts of drawing and quartering, she returns. She is cheerful; a good sign, unless she truly enjoys deporting applicants. Perhaps she's a Tory. But she looks at us and, smiling, beckons us forward.

Our documents are returned. My passport has a nice, new stamp on it. She welcomes me to the UK and we are released to make our way across the sea of humanity toward the exits.

The line of applicants outside the building now stretches around the corner, yet people continue to arrive. We wonder how early the first person in line had to get up, and then decide not to think about it.

It is not yet eleven o'clock but already we feel drained and dazed. Ahead we spy a teashop and decide that my first act as a legal resident of the United Kingdom should be to have some tea and scones. It seems like a grand idea.

The Knights Who
Say "NI"

I am, they assure me, in need of a National Insurance Number.

This came to light while filling out a job application form that made me long for the simplicity and clarity of a 1040 tax booklet. If I'm going to work in the UK, I'm going to need their equivalent of a Social Security Number.

Unfortunately, they don't use NI numbers here quite the same as we use Social Security numbers. My wife could neither tell me what her number was nor figure out where her NI card might be, which left us little to go on. We checked the web without success and then decided to try contacting Inland Revenue on the assumption they might be able to tell us where to go.

I called the local office and, as I had hoped, they told me I was in the wrong place and gave me a number to call. So I called that number.

No one answered.

I tried again, with the same result.

And again.

And again.

So I called the Inland Revenue in a different city, where I was once again told I was connected to the wrong office and given the same phone number I had been fruitlessly calling throughout the bulk of the morning. The lady in this office, however, was kind enough to tell me the name of the office I was trying to contact.

"You need to talk to the 'DSS,'" she said, and hung up.

I looked up DSS in the phone book and found nothing. So I called the number again. Again, no one answered.

At length, I asked my father-in-law if he knew of a 'DSS.'

"Of course," he said. "That's the Department of Social Security. You'd better go down in person, they don't answer their phone."

And so I went into town and located the DSS in an unimaginative civic structure reminiscent of a DMV office complete with benches bolted to the floor. I was told to take a number and wait. And wait. And wait.

When, at last, I was called to a window, I explained my situation. "You can't have an NI number until you get a job," the man told me.

"But the application forms ask for it; I'm going to need one before I start work."

"You can't have an NI number until you get a job."

It was clear I was up against bureaucracy, as stolid and illogical as any the US could produce. I fell back on my usual strategy: begging.

"Please, is there any way I can get a number now?"

He considered my request.

"If you can prove to me that you are currently, actively seeking employment, and have a right to live in the UK, if you have your visa, and documents proving you've signed up with employment agencies and have been on interviews, then I might be able to set you up with an appointment to see if you can get an NI number."

I assured him I had such documents and could return with them. I took the bus back home, spent an hour or so pulling papers from my files and printing e-mails, then raced back to the DSS office and took another number.

And waited.

And waited.

After a while, it was my turn at the window, but my man was busy denying someone else's request.

"I'm here to get an NI number," I began telling the woman at my window. "I was here earlier this afternoon and—"

"Oh, certainly!" she said. "Here, let me fill out this application form. Is next Wednesday good for you? Fine. Just show this to the woman at the reception desk and she'll make the appointment."

"Don't you want to see my documentation?"

"Oh no, we don't need to see any of that."

Since I couldn't reach through the glass to strangle the officious drone in the next cubicle, I had to settle for a vivid, mini-fantasy involving him, a coil of stout rope, a nest of anthills and a large vat of honey while I smiled and thanked the kind woman at my booth.

Now I understand why all the seats are bolted to the floor.

Transitions

One of the strangest side effects of my continental drifting was the fact that, when I checked out of my apartment in the US and bummed a ride to the airport (ironically, with my ex-wife) I was officially homeless. That's not a feeling I'm accustomed to, but there was no denying it; I had nowhere to live, no job and was heading to a place where neither of those comforts awaited me.

After 25 years of gainful employment and semi-responsible home ownership/apartment dwelling, I was suddenly, and quite jarringly, unfettered. I'm not sure how I was supposed to feel about that—perhaps I expected the siren call of the unencumbered life to lure me away to Aruba where I could live out my days as a beach bum—but what I did feel was scared. For those of you who have not had this experience (and for your sakes, I hope that is all of you) looking down and not seeing a net makes you want to wet your pants.

Thankfully, that feeling lasted only until I boarded the plane and my old friend Stark Terror took over. After that, when it became apparent my new in-laws weren't going to let me starve, I eased into my new role as a layabout.

I have since, and in quick succession, become a 'we' and then we acquired an apartment, though my bride insists on calling it a flat. What we have not acquired is furniture.

My wife is the frugal one in this relationship (as well as the only one bringing in the money) but as attractive as the idea of freeloading off my in-laws was, she could foresee a time when having their new son-in-law living in their daughter's bedroom might, one day, wear a little thin and made the decision to move me out while everyone was still on speaking terms. But her splurging on an abode did not include putting anything, aside from us, in it; all we had was an old futon that used to belong to her brother and the 17 crates of household goods I shipped, at great expense, from the US.

The futon worked as a bed for about two nights, after which we decided sleeping on the floor was more comfortable. Now we use the futon as a makeshift settee, having placed it in the middle of the empty living room, facing the picture window, which serves as a sort of large, high-definition, flat-screen television that shows only one program. And since we're on the top floor, that program is mostly blue.

Still, we have a lot to keep us occupied, like sorting through the cartons I mailed over. I'm not sure what happened to them, but somewhere along the way (and Lord knows they had the time), someone took out all of the vitally important, indispensable items I had packed and replaced them with random junk.

Spatulas; did I really believe there was a dearth of flexible, rubber cooking implements in England? And even if there were, would it really have impacted on my lifestyle? And why the six economy-sized bags of Halls Menthol cough drops, the eight cans of shave cream with accompanying packs of Gillette razors (especially when I use an electric shaver), the ash tray or the clothes hangers; what was I thinking? Probably the same thing that prompted me to pack coffee mugs and mixing bowls and measuring cups and potholders and flatware and hand towels and assorted jars of spices. I'm not sure what I thought I was getting into, but it cost more to mail all those items over than it would to buy them at British Home Stores.

But, ill conceived or not, they are all here now, and at least we have a nicely kitted out kitchen. We could also, if we wished, have romantic candlelight dinners with authentic whale-oil candles and brass candlestick holders, even if we don't have a table. And we do get to sleep on Egyptian cotton sheets with matching pillowcases, sans bed.

It's strange, being surrounded by this sporadic opulence while living the life of a refugee; it's like seeing a street person drinking a bottle of Veuve Clicquot wrapped in a brown paper sack.

I'm sure I'll look back on these days with fondness (that's the best way to look at them—in the distant past) for they're about to come to an end. The final foundation stone in my new life has, at last, been fitted into place and we will no longer have to live on love alone. I got a job.

I received the call this morning; a software company in Brighton has decided to pass over a hard-working, native Briton in order to give this immigrant a job. It's half the pay I was making in America, but it's a start. I'm going to celebrate after lunch by walking to Curry's and buying an iron. Then, when my wife gets home, maybe I can convince her to go out shopping for furniture.

The job doesn't start until the end of the month, so we still have a few weeks left of living on love, but perhaps we'll also have a table.

A Typical Day

Mostly, the mornings are gray. Many times, however, the low slate shelf blows over and blue sky, fluffy white clouds and even sunshine are the order of the day. Other times, the drab skies do nothing but hang overhead and brood. Then, of course, it rains.

The next thing you notice is the temperature.

England, when compared to upstate New York, has an agreeable climate. You're unlikely to wake up to find your water pipes frozen or your windows blanketed by snowdrifts, but it does get cool, even in the summers, so a little heat is often appreciated. Unfortunately, the British obsession with conservation and frugality makes this a bit awkward.

Your flat—built sometime during the Eisenhower administration and a stranger to refurbishment—is equipped with storage heaters, which, once turned on, don't give off heat—at least, not immediately. Instead, they wait until electric rates are cheapest, then they begin storing heat. When enough heat has been soaked up, it is slowly released. During the cold season, when the heaters are on continually, this isn't so much of a problem, but if you wake up in the morning to a frigid flat and turn the heater on, you'll have heat the next afternoon, when it's bright and sunny. And you won't be able to stop it. Even if you unplug the heater, it will continue to release the stored heat until it is empty. This can take several days.

Weather and temperature aside, it's time to start your day.

In the bathroom, if you're paying attention, you will notice there is no toilet. The toilet is in another room, all by itself. This can be jarring at first, but it doesn't take long to discover the advantages of such an arrangement.

You'll also notice that the English haven't yet caught on to the concept that hot and cold water, coming out of the same faucet, produces warm water. In the tub and the sink, there are two taps. One is cold, the other, ostensibly, hot, although this depends on the time of day, since the hot water heater is also programmed to turn itself on only when electric rates are low.

In the morning, you will note, it is hot—scalding even—which necessitates moving your hands rapidly back and forth between the hot and cold taps. You could use the small rubber bung chained to the sink to stop up the drain and fill the sink with warm water, but having been raised on the single-tap method, this doesn't occur to you.

After applying burn ointment to your hands, you search in vain for a place to plug in your electric razor. You needn't bother. First of all, if you have a US razor, you can't plug it in anywhere. The two or three pronged plugs common in the US look positively petit next to the honking big plugs on the British appliances. Their plugs have to be big—they draw 220 volts, not 110. If you did manage to plug a US razor into a UK socket, it would explode. This makes the Brits very cautious around electricity.

But 220 or 110, US or UK, you still can't run your razor in the bathroom. There are no plugs.

This is a safety feature, based on the premise that electricity and water don't mix. The net result is a national paucity of amusing anecdotes involving hair driers and showers, but the Brits seem willing to sacrifice a bit of humor for the sake of aggregate longevity.

With no plug or switches allowed in the bathroom, what you do have are "pullies," or pull strings, which turn on the light, the heater and the shower.

The light—okay, you've probably got that one figured out—but the heater and the shower may require some explanation. High up on the wall (you can locate it by looking at the other end of one of the pullies) is a longish, metal device that looks like a florescent light fixture with a metal rod where the bulb should be. Pull the string and the rod soon starts to glow red, bathing your scalp in harsh heat. This is your bathroom heater. It is the only heating appliance, aside from the stove, which you can turn on and receive instant gratification. Remember this in December.

Unlike the heater, the shower and its pull string are nowhere near each other, and the shower will not work until you turn it on. Look for a seemingly random string hanging from the ceiling. Over there, in the corner, that's the one. Pull it and you'll see a little red light come on. Okay, now the shower is activated.

The shower itself is a cunning device—a box, mounted on the wall above the tub, which takes in cold water and spews tepid water out of a showerhead. It's a grand idea, though it does not produce anything your average American would mistake for actual water pressure.

After your shower, you notice something that looks like a scale, but with strange numbers on it. These are stones and kilograms.

Stones are relatively easy to deal with; you can convert them by multiplying by 14. For example: If the scale reads 10 stone 3, then you weigh 14 times 10 plus 3, or 143 pounds. (Note that the scale does not actually read 10 stone 3, you only wish it did.) That may seem like a lot of mental math to ask of your brain this early in the morning, but it's easier than trying to convert kilograms—for that, I recommend a calculator.

Back in the bedroom, you look for a closet and a suitable outlet for your razor. You find neither. In Britain, there are no closets; clothing is kept in something that looks like an oversized gun cabinet,

176

which they call a wardrobe. And the outlets in the rest of the apartment are for normal, three pronged plugs, while your razor has a two pronged safety plug for the type of outlet you would have found in your bathroom if electrical outlets had been allowed in bathrooms when your flat was built, which they weren't.

If you want to plug your razor in, you'll need an adapter, which you can pick up at any hardware store.

Time for breakfast. The kitchen is smaller than what you are used to, but not small enough to take much notice of. What you do find notable are the diminutive appliances.

Yes, those small, white boxes underneath the kitchen counter are the refrigerator, the freezer and the washing machine. Added to this line-up is a kitchen stove which looks like something a 10-year old might get for Christmas; you are certain, if you look closely, you will find the words "Easy-Bake" embossed on it somewhere.

Let's start with the fridge. Think back—what do you consider the best years of your life? Most people say their college years, when you lived in a dorm room and had a tiny refrigerator in the corner. Welcome back to the best years of your life!

But seriously, isn't your American fridge crammed with a lot of junk you're never going to use; RubberMaid™ containers housing furry or otherwise suspicious looking items that used to be food, a bottle of wine you got for your 32nd birthday even though you don't like wine, the brown, shriveled spheroid in the bottom drawer (next to the wilted broccoli and manky carrots) that used to be a head of lettuce back when you bought it on impulse, thinking it was time you started eating better? If you got rid of all that stuff, you'd find a small fridge like this one has ample room for real food and keeps you from accumulating a lot of junk. And the freezer, which is as big as the fridge, is actually larger than your American freezer, so quit your bitching.

You might wish the washing machine was a little bit bigger, but if you did wash a big American-sized load of laundry, how are you going to dry it all? You can't dry more than six items at a time on the clotheshorse in the hall without the law of diminishing returns kicking in.

Now open the fridge and get out some breakfast. The food is edible enough, but you won't find much you recognize. Even the eggs look a little, shall we say, different (here's a hint—wash them). Don't panic, just pick out some things you think you can deal with (suggestion: cheese, milk and the aforementioned eggs) and get on with it.

Before you start cooking, it's worth mentioning that the US is years ahead of the UK in terms of non-stick technology, so make liberal use of butter or cooking oil.

Breakfast over; it's time to learn about doing the dishes, or washing up, UK style. First, fill the sink with hot water and dish soap, then immerse your dishes and wash them as you normally would. Now take them out of the soapy water and put them in the drying rack. No, no, don't rinse them; just put them in the rack. Yes, like that, with soap bubbles all over them. Apparently, your mother was wrong—you can eat off dishes that have not been thoroughly rinsed and not get sick. In time you'll get used to the idea. (Or you can sneak back into the kitchen and rinse them off when no one is looking.)

You're well into your day now and should be getting on with your chores. You need to go out to buy that adapter for your razor and you could use more eggs and milk. The sky is blue, the sun is shining and it looks like a grand day for a walk; better take your waterproof jacket.

Walking in England is hard work. In America, folks pass on the right because they drive on the right, so one might expect the Brits to walk the way they drive, even if it is the wrong way around. But instead, they march headlong down narrow sidewalks with no notice of people coming toward them. If you are walking arm-in-arm with someone, it is not unusual for people to walk between you. Every approach is a contest of wills, a guessing game and/or a collision.

Come to think of it, perhaps they do walk the way they drive. As if to prove this, you suddenly find yourself facing an oncoming car. You quickly double-check to assure yourself that you are, indeed, on the sidewalk. This is a tricky business, seeing as how, in Britain, the sidewalk is the pavement, not the street, so when someone shouts, "Walk on the pavement," you're not really certain where to go. But the Brits aren't confused about it, and that is definitely a car and it is definitely on the sidewalk.

No need to panic, just step out of the way and let it go by.

In a country as small and crowded as Britain, traffic, even in a small village, is bound to be an issue. The roads don't help. The one in front of you is about as wide as a narrow, one-way street in the States, but here a commuter bus and a delivery van are inching past each other in opposite directions while an impatient young man on a motorcycle roars between them. This type of traffic is certain to cause tie-ups. Fortunately, the cars are small and fit neatly on the sidewalks.

You wonder if some sort of parking regulation might help the traffic congestion but look in vain for any "No Parking" signs. In fact, there doesn't appear to be many signs at all. The reason is it doesn't snow here, so traffic signs can be painted on the roadway itself to keep the sign-clutter to a minimum. For example: a double yellow line along the side of the road means "No Parking at any Time." You can see it very clearly there, underneath all those parked cars.

After a short but eventful walk, you arrive at the supermarket. The first and most obvious difference is that all four of the shopping cart wheels swivel, making them sort of fun to push around, but aside from that—

and some odd brand names and unusual food items—it's much like an American supermarket. Well, a mid-sized American supermarket. Then you discover the other, glaring difference; they're out of eggs. They're also out of milk.

Back outside, it's raining. Put on your waterproof.

It won't do you any good to ask directions to the nearest hardware store, as there are no hardware stores in England. What they have are DIY stores.

DIY (or, Do It Yourself) is a British obsession. This stems from having small houses, which, even if they are not ancient, seem to be in constant need of some sort of enhancement. The drive to wring more and more space out of tiny living areas is a national mania, so DIY shops are common and generally stocked full of useful items. And DIY doesn't stop inside the house; gardening is also an obsession of the British, who have elevated the practice of creating intricate gardens on plots of land too small to raise veal on into an art form.

So ask anyone where the nearest DIY is and they'll tell you there's a good one just around the corner and up East Street a ways that you can easily walk to. And you head off, not realizing that Brits walk *way* more than we do.

About two and a half miles later, you spot the DIY. On the door is a sign reading, "Closed for Lunch, Noon to 2PM."

It's stopped raining and the sun is shining, so take off your waterproof.

No sense walking all the way back to town, you might as well wait here for the store to reopen. All you need to do is find a pub. This will be easy. One of the best things about Britain is you can't swing a cat without hitting a pub. In fact, there's one next door to the DIY and another one right across the street. Pick one that suits you and settle in.

Since you're not wearing cowboy boots and a ten-gallon hat and smoking a big cigar, people probably won't take you for an American, providing you don't:

- talk too much or too loudly
- leave money lying on the bar
- try to tip the bartender
- refer to the game on the television set as "soccer."

Well, it's two o'clock now and the DIY's open but it's comfortable in here and there's no hurry, so let's have another pint.

And another.

DING! DING! DING!

Hey, what's with the bell? What do you mean I have to drink up and leave? You're closing a perfectly fine pub at 3 o'clock in the afternoon? What on earth for?

They now know you're an American. You're back on the street. It's three thirty in the afternoon and you still haven't shaved.

And it's raining; put on your waterproof.

Sex & the Single Brit

It's taken a while for all of the clues to come together, but after exploring the surrounding towns and countryside, both on foot and by car, it has belatedly occurred to me to ask, "What do British teenagers do for sex?"

I'm not naïve, I realize that, unlike a tsunami, a hormone-enhanced teenager is an unstoppable force, so I know there's shagging going on out there somewhere, I just don't know how. I suppose I could ask some of the local teenagers hanging around the High Street, but that might lead to unfortunate articles about me in the local papers and/or an undesired tour of the British penal system. Besides, that would take the fun out of all this speculation.

But think about it, there's not a drive-in movie theatre in sight and the streets and lanes display a remarkable dearth of roadside motels—you know, the kind that rent rooms by the hour—so where do they go?

There are a good number of B&B's about, but that's the last place you'd want to have an illicit tryst in. Imagine being a hopeful, horny teenager and taking your girlfriend on the bus three towns away to the Strangled Goose only to be greeted at the door by Mrs. Bumfry—whose husband, Goddard, is on the same lawn bowls team as Mr. Wentworth-Hedgerow, whose wife works at the local lending library where your mum volunteers three days a week helping pensioners puzzle out their e-mail—and trying to convince her that you and your "wife" are really Mr. & Mrs. Jack Smitherson from Lower Sheepdip.

And let's say you could get in; a B&B isn't exactly as anonymous as a motel, where you can duck in and out at will in relative anonymity. At a B&B, you'd have to face a gauntlet of knowing looks from the proprietor and the other guests; in general, it's not a place where you want to leave soiled linen.

I could happily assume they rely on that old standby, the car, if it weren't for the fact that you can fit the average British automobile in the boot of most American cars. I know I'm getting old—anything smaller than a Winnebago wouldn't cut it for me these days—but my mind seizes up trying to calculate the calisthenics required to successfully copulate in a Mini. I can only imagine an increasingly frustrated bloke who can't get out of the car until he gets out of the mood, a young lady with a satisfied smile on her face and a middle aged mum doing her weekly Tesco run the next morning wondering why the gearshift is so sticky.

The great outdoors? As an ex-New Yorker, I balk at this idea, but must confess that, in England, the idea may have some merit. First of all the "season" is much longer. Back in the States, the guideline was "Hurray, hurray, the first of May, outdoor humping starts today," but in Britain, especially in the south, it's agreeably warm throughout much of the year. As long as you've got your wellies and a waterproof blanket handy, you should do fine. And despite the high population density, any mildly adventurous couple is bound to discover some remote corner of a wood not frequented by adults, or at least their parents.

Granted, they might be spotted making the two-backed beast by a random hill-walker, but reliable identification is unlikely unless they interrupt to ask directions. ("Excuse me but I seem to be a bit muddled here. Could you tell me if this is the way to Little Pigsty?")

The real downside to this is that it has recently become illegal. That's right, you can no longer be outdoors in the buff in Britain without risking arrest. While this isn't likely to impinge on my lifestyle, I regard it as a silly law and suspect the impetus behind it came, at least partially, from a politically active group of suspicious mothers. Who else would want it that badly? Was stumbling over amorous naturists that much of a problem for the Ramblers Association that they needed a law against it? Or are the local councils hoping to raise revenues by charging admission to the identity parades?

And so I'm left to wonder, about that, and how lap dancers and chip-n-dales can possibly make a living in this country. Given the inborn British resistance to tipping, I can't imagine them willingly putting a lengthwise crease in a five-pound note and sticking it down some stranger's G-string. Even in America, that's a lot of money.

Do strippers give change here? Are they required by law to wear change pouches so they can accept 20 pence pieces and give out handfuls of coins in return for fivers? I'm struggling to visualize a woman trying to pluck up a pound coin while holding her hands behind her back and I find I simply don't want to go there.

I suppose, since none of these activities hold any relevance in my life any longer, I shouldn't be so concerned. But then, you never know, I might want to buff up my six-pack and start a second career as a Chip-n-Dale after I retire.

The Name Game

People in Britain name their houses.

The reasons behind this quaint custom are rooted deep in Britain's history, beginning with the Roman conquest. One of the many changes the Romans imposed upon Britain was a system of numbering houses. This made deliveries easier for their Postal Carriers and worked fine until the Romans left, at which time life became suddenly difficult for the Anglo-Saxon Posties, who could only scratch their heads over addresses like Romvlvs, CCDLXIV Mead Street, Winchester before tossing the letters in the gutter.

Shortly after that, everybody forgot how to read and things got a little easier.

When the Normans invaded, William the Conqueror wanted a full accounting of his new country and insisted that houses be labeled alphabetically within each street by their owner's name. This led to much shifting about of households and required squeezing, for instance, Peter's new house between Oswald and Ralph (there were no names that began with "Q" in those days). This is why British homes are so tiny and cramped together and why Aaron and Lloyd are spelled that way.

Obviously, this method didn't work very well and fell out of favor as soon as William died, after which the locals returned to their original houses.

This confused the Norman Posties—who had replaced the Anglo-Saxon Posties—so much they passed a law calling for a new system of household identification involving actual numbers. But, since the Normans were French, no one could understand the new law and everyone simply renamed their homes as they saw fit.

Eventually a numbering system was imposed (this was under Henry the VIII, who had invented a numeric classification scheme to keep track of his wives), but by then, the custom of naming houses was deeply ingrained.

Even today, as you walk down any street, you will note that a high percentage of homes have a plaque of some sort affixed to their gate, front wall, or, in the case of the tiny Victorian row houses, hanging above their door. The names can be mysterious (Dragons), whimsical (I ♥ my villa), functional (Toll Cottage, on what used to be, one must assume, a toll cottage), redundant (Brick House, in a land where nearly every dwelling is made of brick), trendy (Greensleeves), cute (Dorabill, on the home of Dora and Bill), punny (Maidenover—which, I am told, is a Cricket term—on a house in Cricket Field Road) or just plain strange (Brilig, Dunragit).

But, in each case, I must assume that some amount of thought went into the naming and that the plaques, large or small, reflect the pride of homeownership in a land where housing is scarce and dear.

I think it's a lovely custom, and so I've decided to name our flat.

As with the homeowners, a lot of thought went into the name but, unlike them, my plaque won't be an ornate sign affixed to a wrought iron gate. It will, instead, be a small plate, Blu-Tacked below the Judas hole of a rented, 2nd-floor walk-up.

My wife thinks the idea is incredibly naff, and so do I, but then, that's the point.

After much discussion, we chose a name alluding to the way my wife and I met, crossbred with some lyrics

186

from the Sting song, "Fields of Gold," which would be considered "our" song, if we had a song, which we don't.

In order to accomplish this melding, the English lyrics had to be translated into Irish Gaelic. This wasn't difficult—the Internet is awash in translation dictionaries, everything from Abenaki to Zulu. No, the problem was the result.

Orgagort.

We rolled that around in our heads for a few days but couldn't get past the notion that it sounded like something you'd go to the doctor's to get a shot of penicillin to cure.

My wife suggested translating it into Scottish Gaelic, but what's the point in that? We didn't meet in Scotland. I might just as well translate it into Danish. Besides, the outcome might be even more horrible.

In the end, we decided the original English sounded best: Goldenfields.

So if you ever come to visit my "estate" you may make note of the nameplate and even comment on how unusual it is for a flat to have a name, but don't bother telling me how naff it is. I already know.

I Just Don't Get It

Men, I've heard it said, are like bears with furniture. Left to our own devices, we would never come up with the concept of bed ruffles, doilies, matching towel sets or even curtains. That's what women are for.

Once introduced to the niceties of civilization, however, many of us recognize the advantages and willingly embrace them. Over the years, I have learned to appreciate theatre, classic art, fine wine and 300 thread-count Egyptian cotton sheets, to name but a few, and each has enriched my life in ways I could not have imagined. The one product of civilization that continues to elude me is classical music.

I'm sorry, but I just don't get it.

Sure, it's complex and thematic and all that but unless I recognize the melody from a Bugs Bunny cartoon, they all sound the same to me.

Despite having learned to appreciate the subtle variations between sipping Pinot Grigio out of a crystal wine glass and guzzling Blue Nun from a Flintstones jelly jar, I remain, despite repeated introductions, unable to embrace the nuances of Rock Monnanoff in quite the same way as the latest Oasis CD.

There's something there, I'm certain of it. (Either that, or the entire classical music movement was begun and propagated solely as a grand practical joke on people like me). Listening to classical music makes the aficionado feel good, similar to the lift I get from seeing matching curtains in my sitting room instead of an old blanket I found in the tire-well of my car.

Whenever I attend a concert, there is always some guy who leaps to his feet the moment the orchestra stops playing to shout, "BRAVO!" and begin a wave of enthusiastic applause. I want to understand what he is feeling, I really do, but I can't get past the idea that Rigatoni's Piñata Concerto in E Flat Minor has little more to offer than the opportunity for a satisfying nap. I mean, some of these pieces last forty-five minutes; and I used to think In-A-Gadda-Da-Vida was long.

During my most recent exposure to culture, I stumbled upon a method of, if not appreciating the music, at least maintaining my attention. We were at a concert in London, and I happened to have with me a small set of binoculars (but that's another story). From my perch in the balcony, the mass of black and white and various bits of wood on the stage suddenly came alive as proximity transformed it from an anonymous homogony spewing unintelligible music, to individual people, each contributing their talents to the whole, by spewing unintelligible music.

I panned from section to section, picking out each musician as they sawed away at strings, blew into a variety of brass or woodwind instruments, or tapped away at the glockenspiel. Their faces were studies of concentration but, between numbers, they chatted with their neighbors like punters around the office cooler. It was strange to think that, while I was enjoying my free time, they were in the middle of their workday, and I wondered how well I would perform if they all came to my office and stood in front of my desk to watch me organize an expense report.

The women's attire consisted mainly of low cut or sleeveless evening wear and every one of them possessed smooth, white, unblemished skin, leaving me to ponder the odds of ever again finding that many people dressed in black together in one place without a facial piercing or visible tattoo among them. The orchestral society obviously has a very strict dress code.

What would happen, I wondered, if one of them got drunk one night (do classical musicians party—I mean in the way you and I party; not the type of party where tastefully dressed teenagers proffer silver trays artfully arranged with tiny sandwiches and cut-glass bud vases half-filled with low-octane champagne) and woke up to find a bicep sporting a skull and cross bones festooned with a scroll reading "Born to Raise Handel?" Would they be drummed out of the service, their violin bow ceremoniously broken and tossed out after them? And how could someone, so bereft of actual life skills, hope to earn a living?

This leads me to question if any of the supplicating disenfranchised I cross London's narrow lanes to avoid might once have had promising careers as concert violinists, only to be disqualified due to a nose ring violation.

It was gratifying to discover that the novelty value of peering down the bodice of the London Philharmonic Orchestra's second cello was enough to see me through the bulk of Muscateli's Sangria for Picante in B#. Before I knew it, the music stopped, the cellist leaned forward to close her book and someone in the next section leapt to his feet to shout "BRAVO!"

It occurred to me then that this guy might not actually have a superior appreciation of music; maybe he just has a better pair of binoculars.

A Coventry Carol

C oventry: the name itself has a quaint and vaguely medieval sound, conjuring up images of ancient cathedrals surrounded by stone cottages, pristine snow, the smell of wood smoke and bands of rosy-cheeked ragamuffins in floppy scarves singing Christmas carols. I admit this painfully romantic image results from nothing more than the yuletide song "Coventry Carol" (of which I know neither the words nor the tune), but that was enough to promote this midlands town onto my mental list of mystical cities along with (though somewhere below) Paris, Blackpool and Timbuktu.

I visited Coventry yesterday. It was just a drive-thru (actually, it was a ride-thru, as I wasn't driving). We were three hours into a normally three-and-a-half-hour journey home from Birmingham, having managed only 20 miles, and were no closer to our destination than when we started. We didn't mean to go there, but we had no choice; it was the only place in England where traffic was moving.

The events that led us there began, unbeknown to us, during the afternoon while we were meeting with clients. When the day ended, we headed to the motorway (the UK equivalent of Interstate Highway System, except they don't have states here and calling them Intershires would sound a bit pretentious and wouldn't be fair to Devon, Suffolk and all the other shire-less counties) and found they had closed Britain. The reason: wind.

Now, I'm a big fan of England, but I am coming to the conclusion that it doesn't require much to bring the British Empire to its knees. Mainly, all you need is weather; any kind will do. Too cold and the roads ice up, too hot, they buckle, too wet, they disappear into a quagmire, and now, too windy and things fall over, including big trucks. Keeping in mind that a well-timed auto accident can make three-quarters of the population late for dinner, you'll appreciate that it doesn't require a major disruption of the traffic infrastructure to bring the entire country to a standstill.

To try to visualize the ensuing chaos, imagine New Jersey at rush hour with the Garden State Parkway, the New Jersey Turnpike and, just for added spice, sections of I-287 and the Lincoln Tunnel closed. Now imagine this Gordian Knot of snarled traffic spread over an area the size of, well, New Jersey.

We sat stock-still in southbound traffic for over an hour, then decided traveling north would be a better option because it offered the off-chance of movement and access to a service station (to provide sustenance for our thirsty vehicle). We did, eventually, find a gas station, but stationary traffic forced us to do some off-roading in order to reach it.

Having arrived at a semi-decongested area, we stocked up for a long drive and reconnoitered an alternate route home; one that took us through Coventry. I decided to look forward to that as an alternative to exploring the suddenly alluring adventure of suicide by means of my tongue and the car's dashboard cigarette lighter.

And so, we went to Coventry.

(Aside: during the standard research I did for this chapter—which involves telling my wife about it and hoping she has some pithy observations to contribute—I learned about being "sent to Coventry," as opposed to simply ending up there accidentally, as we did.)

Now, these were clearly not the best of circumstances for sightseeing, so I'm not saying Coventry isn't a lovely place, but to me, it simply looked wet, gray and dreary. There were no quaint buildings or cherub-faced children or fresh fallen snow (it is the middle of January, for pity's sake). The only glitter I saw involved streetlights reflecting off the rain-slicked concrete.

As everyone else in a 150-mile radius remained trapped in the traffic cluster surrounding Birmingham, we made it through the city center in a remarkably short time and were soon heading, with palpable relief, southward on the M-40.

Until we hit yet another traffic jam.

By now, it was nearly 9 PM. With nothing but stationary traffic to look forward to, I sipped some water, looked out the window at the dark and sodden countryside and tried not to think about the cigarette lighter.

Winter

Has anyone else noticed that sleeping with your secretary at the office Christmas party is a perfect metaphor for the Holiday season as a whole? I didn't think so, but hear me out anyway.

First there is the overall event, filled with glitter, good cheer and lots of drunken hugging. Add to that the pervasive promise of presents, the excited expectation of secrets soon to be revealed, and you're practically bursting with excitement when the affair finally comes to a head. Then, in a brief, orgiastic frenzy, everything is unwrapped and opened, fondled and forgotten or eaten and drunk until, sated, you look around at the evidence of your excess and feel a rising sense of guilt. You begin to wonder where your resolutions vanished to and now wish the whole thing would just go away and let you get on with your life, or at least stop calling you at two o'clock in the morning in a weepy, drunken stupor.

(Allow me to state, for the record, that I do not have a secretary and have, therefore, not slept with one; I am making these suppositions based on the observations of those people who do and did.)

The accumulation of days now pushing Christmas further and further behind us serve only as a nagging reminder that, A) it's now merely winter, and B) I haven't taken down my Christmas decorations yet. We're currently entering what I like to call the underbelly of the year, that ragged seam between the festive season and the arrival of spring; a time when getting up would be the hardest part of your day provided the rest of the day wasn't so crappy.

All of this is the long way of saying I have those mid-winter blues, and, while I have often remarked (to the irritation of those I left behind in the Great White Northeast) that winters in England are nowhere near as harsh as they are in upstate New York, they are God-awful dark. In addition to that, the British climate makes full use of what little cold it does produce and has, through centuries of diligent practice, long ago perfected the art of seeping into your bones and sucking your soul out through your nostrils. (Even so, I still wouldn't trade a winter here for one in Albany, but I wouldn't mind swapping with someone in, say, Barcelona.)

Winter in England means evening, like an inconsiderate dinner guest, arrives several hours early, when you're dusted with flour, making the hors d'oeuvres and haven't stepped into the shower yet, while Dawn, the little tart, doesn't sneak in until most responsible people have already started their day, and even then can't be bothered to offer a suitable explanation. The few daylight hours occurring between these events tend to be muted by low clouds, dispiriting drizzle and the occasional, sad attempt at sleet.

And, to make things worse, all around me I see remnants of the erstwhile festive season—languishing decorations, dead, discarded trees and rubbish bins overflowing with shredded ribbons, crumpled wrapping paper and empty beer bottles—which, like the aforementioned secretary, seem determined to hang around even though they no longer have the capacity to inspire joy and serve only as a reminder of our brief, and perhaps misguided, frivolity.

I guess that means I've come full circle and, though I still have more to say on the subject, I suppose I ought to let you off so you can get back to the business of enduring winter. Besides, I think it's about time I took those decorations down.

Postcards From Across the Pond

and

More Postcards From Across the Pond

Are available on:
Amazon.com, Amazon.co.uk
and other retailers

http://michaelharling.com
Sussex, United Kingdom

Made in the USA
Las Vegas, NV
08 January 2023

65234377R00121